"Stress is part of life for any teen—but Jeffrey Bernstein's new book, *The Stress* proven tools for making you feel more happier."

—**Mark Bertin, MD**, developmental pediatrician, and author of *How Children Thrive and Mindful Parenting for ADHD*

"I loved Jeffrey Bernstein's integration of cognitive behavioral therapy (CBT) practices with positive psychology—two powerful sets of practices to help you deal with the stresses of being a teen in the twenty-first century. The principles you learn here can help you not only survive the challenges of your teenage years, but will be invaluable skills as you transition to the demands of adulthood."

—**Seth Gillihan, PhD**, creator of the *Think Act Be* podcast and blog, author of *The CBT Deck*, and coauthor of *A Mindful Year*

"*The Stress Survival Guide for Teens* provides valuable tools to help teens decrease their stress. Jeffrey Bernstein has created exercises that combine CBT and positive psychology that are fun and engaging. I would highly recommend this book to teens and those who work with teens. Looking forward to using this workbook with my clients!"

—**Caren Baruch-Feldman, PhD**, psychologist, and author of *The Grit Guide for Teens*

"As with his other books, Jeff Bernstein's most recent offering, *The Stress Survival Guide for Teens*, takes on an important issue that directly affects the lives of many adolescents and their families. Bernstein not only describes the common problems, but also provides page after page of clear and thorough guidance for what to do about them. He delivers the tried-and-true skills for facing and handling the many pressures and worries of adolescence in a manner that will leave readers feeling as though they are sitting across from an expert who really 'gets it.'"

—**J. Russell Ramsay, PhD**, associate professor in the department of clinical psychology, and codirector of the Perelman School of Medicine's Adult ADHD Treatment and Research Program at the University of Pennsylvania; and author of *The Adult ADHD Tool Kit* and *Rethinking Adult ADHD*

"Wow! What a relevant book in this age of increasing anxiety with today's youth. With Jeff's many years working with young people on mental health issues, he has collected the best of techniques to help children gain control over their emotions! This book is a great resource for any child dealing with anxiety! It is also a 'must-have' for school counselors!"

—**Carol DeMarco, MSW**, middle school counselor for twenty years at Peirce Middle School in West Chester, PA

"Jeffrey Bernstein's latest book teaches teens of all ages important cognitive-behavioral and positive psychology skills to help equip them to handle the roller-coaster ride of life. This is a practical, easy-to-read, relatable, and highly recommended resource to put teens into the driver's seat of the stressful and emotional highs and lows, and challenging twists and turns of adolescence that are an inevitable part of growing up."

> —**Stephanie Margolese, PhD**, clinical psychologist; associate professor in the department of psychiatry, and assistant professor in the department of psychology at McGill University; and author of *My Brain Team* and *Sam's Big Secret*

"Bernstein's wisdom is on point in *The Stress Survival Guide for Teens*. I heartily recommend this skills-based book for anyone wanting to reduce their stress, gain control in their life, and learn to put the brakes on the difficulties that come with being a teen. For professionals, the combination of CBT, mindfulness, and positive psychology practices make this a complete tool kit for assisting clients. For teens and young adults, this practical guide provides accessible examples for getting a handle on and taming your stress."

> —**Gina M. Biegel, MA, LMFT**, psychotherapist; researcher; author and coauthor of several books, including *The Mindfulness Workbook for Self-Harm*, *The Stress Reduction Workbook for Teens*, and *Be Mindful Card Deck for Teens*; founder of the Mindfulness-Based Stress Reduction for Teens (MBSR-T) program; and CEO of Stressed Teens

"Let's face it, today's teens face more challenges and experience more stress than at any other time in modern history. The realities of a fast-paced digital world leave many feeling chronically anxious, and at times, emotionally and physically overwhelmed. *The Stress Survival Guide for Teens* provides practical, easy-to-understand, research-supported tools to cope with the mounting pressures of teen life. Although a self-help book written specifically for teens, this is a valuable resource for parents, school personnel, and clinicians."

> —**Roger K. McFillin, PsyD, ABPP**, executive director at the Center for Integrated Behavioral Health, board certified in behavioral and cognitive psychology, and coauthor of *Specialty Competencies in Clinical Psychology*

"Teenagers today live in a modern world filled with stress and uncertainty. In *The Stress Survival Guide for Teens*, Jeffrey Bernstein expertly delivers clinical wisdom to help teens cope with life stressors using a unique blend of CBT and positive psychology that is both personal yet practical—a highly effective guide for teenagers, parents, and clinicians alike!"

> —**Shannon Delaney, MD**, child and adolescent psychiatrist, and assistant professor at Columbia University Medical Center

the *i*nstant help
solutions series

Young people today need mental health resources more than ever. That's why New Harbinger created the **Instant Help Solutions Series** especially for teens. Written by leading psychologists, physicians, and professionals, these evidence-based self-help books offer practical tips and strategies for dealing with a variety of mental health issues and life challenges teens face, such as depression, anxiety, bullying, eating disorders, trauma, and self-esteem problems.

Studies have shown that young people who learn healthy coping skills early on are better able to navigate problems later in life. Engaging and easy-to-use, these books provide teens with the tools they need to thrive—at home, at school, and on into adulthood.

This series is part of the **New Harbinger Instant Help Books** imprint, founded by renowned child psychologist Lawrence Shapiro. For a complete list of books in this series, visit newharbinger.com.

the stress survival guide for teens

cbt skills to worry less, develop grit & live your best life

JEFFREY BERNSTEIN, PhD

Instant Help Books
An Imprint of New Harbinger Publications, Inc.

Publisher's Note

Distributed in Canada by Raincoast Books

Copyright © 2019 by Jeffrey Bernstein
     Instant Help Books
     An Imprint of New Harbinger Publications, Inc.
     5674 Shattuck Avenue
     Oakland, CA 94609
     www.newharbinger.com

Cover design by Amy Shoup

Acquired by Elizabeth Hollis Hansen

Edited by Will DeRooy

FSC
www.fsc.org
MIX
Paper from
responsible sources
FSC® C011935

Library of Congress Cataloging-in-Publication Data on file

Printed in the United States of America

21 20 19

10 9 8 7 6 5 4 3 2 1   First Printing

Contents

To the countless teens who live the wisdom of the fictitious boxer, Rocky Balboa: "It ain't about how hard you hit. It's about how hard you can get hit and keep moving forward."

Introduction

Managing Stress to Feel Happier

Stress is an unfortunate reality for nearly all teens. And teens in this fast-paced digital age may be under more stress than any other generation of youths in recent history. Believe me when I say that, by comparison, your parents had it easy!

Many different aspects of a young person's life can be stressful. Maybe right now you're super-worried about an upcoming test. Maybe a good friend of yours has been acting strange and you're not sure what the deal is. Perhaps you're being left out of group texts or your social-media feed isn't getting the likes it used to. Maybe your well-intended parents keep asking you questions but just don't seem to understand what makes you tick. To be totally fair, maybe *you're* still trying to figure out what makes you tick.

Whenever stress hits, you might feel really overwhelmed, worried, irritable, or sad. You might find yourself trying to avoid these feelings by watching videos or playing games on your phone every chance you get. Maybe you lash out at your parents (or your brother or sister) without meaning to (after all, you're only human, right?). Perhaps you vent about your stress to your friends, but after a while they don't seem to want to listen anymore, which is frustrating in itself. Or maybe you just want to sleep so that you don't have to deal with anyone or anything. Unmanaged stress can take a big-time toll on your physical and emotional health. At the same time, there's a lot of fun to be had as a teenager. Right now, there are probably some very exciting experiences and opportunities opening up for you.

This book uses the metaphor of a roller coaster to help you understand stress, because the ups and downs of teenage life can really make you feel like you're soaring one minute and plummeting the next. With the help of this book, you can learn some super-valuable tools to help you feel less stressed and more happy overall. You'll discover powerful ways to lower your stress and feel more in control of your life. Once you learn how to manage stress, you'll feel better and be more able to handle both the routine and the unexpected demands of being a teenager. Reading this book won't stop you from ever getting stressed out ever again. But once you begin to use the stress-management skills described in it, you just might find that lowering your stress is much easier than you imagined.

Cognitive Behavioral Therapy and Positive Psychology to the Rescue

One way this book will help you is by teaching you strategies from cognitive behavioral therapy (also known as CBT). A second set of skills you'll learn comes from what's known as positive psychology. Both CBT and positive psychology are filled with tools that have been proven to lower people's stress.

Many teens, when life gets challenging, find themselves being whisked along by upsetting and negative thoughts. These thoughts seem to get faster and scarier at every turn. If this ever happens to you, it may feel as though you're on a roller coaster, and not the safe, fun kind you find in an amusement park! Roller coasters need brakes to keep them from getting out of hand, and so does your stressed teenage brain. You'll learn to use CBT skills as your main brake lever. Your second brake lever, positive psychology, will help you see and appreciate the good things within you and in your life.

The essence of CBT involves challenging your stress-related, upsetting thoughts with more realistic, healthier thoughts. As you practice CBT skills, you'll see how changing your *thoughts* changes your *feelings*, and this helps you change your *behaviors*. Let's say you're riddled with anxiety about your upcoming dance audition. How awesome would it be to transform those thoughts that are plaguing you, such as *I'll bomb out at this audition!* into ones that help you feel more confident about it and encourage you to practice so that you can truly do your best on stage?

And positive psychology, for its part, is about looking at what's already going in your favor and then using that to feel better. As you'll learn, positive psychology includes seeing your strengths, learning how to become more optimistic, gaining grit, finding flow (kind of like being "in the zone"), and having gratitude. Grit and resilience are similar, but there is an important distinction. *Resilience* is the ability to adapt in the face of stress, in times of hardship, or in light of bad past experiences. Meanwhile, *grit* is the determination to keep working toward your dreams and develop the skills you need to accomplish even the toughest goals.

How to Get the Most from This Book

In the first part of this book (chapters 1 to 3), you'll learn what stress is, what impact it has on *you*, and how it can turn you into your own worst enemy. You'll gain a basic understanding of CBT and positive psychology and learn how to tune in to your body to listen to its stress signals so that you'll know just when to use these powerful tools in day-to-day life.

Part 2 (chapters 4 and 5) and part 3 (chapters 6 and 7), respectively, will provide you with more in-depth CBT and positive psychology skills. You'll use CBT strategies and activities to practice identifying, evaluating, and replacing the thoughts that stress you out. Then we'll talk about what makes you a valuable person, keeping a positive outlook, handling setbacks, getting into the moment, and feeling gratitude. Part 4 (chapters 8 through 10) will let you practice applying your new CBT and positive psychology skills to three huge roller coasters in any teen's life: school pressures, relationship stressors, and family friction. Finally, the conclusion to this book will help you set your mind to managing stress for the rest of your life.

Throughout this book are sections called "In Their Own Words." The quotes in these sections reflect views that teens have expressed to me in my counseling practice (although their names have been changed to protect their confidentiality). Every chapter also includes hands-on activities (under the heading "Try This!") to teach you simple but highly effective stress-management skills. Finally, worksheets for you to fill in, and an audio recording of an exercise in chapter 2, are available for download at the website for this book, http://www.newharbin ger.com/43911. (See the very back of this book for more details.)

Teens Are My Teachers as Well as My Clients

My knowledge about teen stress management comes from the best source available—teens themselves. Having been a child and teen psychologist for more than thirty years, I've learned firsthand which strategies offer the most relief to teens who are feeling overwhelmed, frustrated, and even miserable. The CBT and positive psychology tools in this book are the very same approaches that have worked for the more than three thousand teens I've talked to. Although there are many approaches to lowering stress, my teen clients have repeatedly told me that CBT and positive psychology offer very powerful, quick, and easy-to-use stress-melting strategies. My previous book, *Mindfulness for Teen Worry*, teaches valuable mindfulness skills, which can help reduce your stress too. After reading this one, you might want to check it out.

I'm excited for you to learn how you can manage the nagging and weighty stress that makes so many teens feel terrible. I'm confident that the tools and strategies you gain from this book can help you feel calmer and happier throughout your life.

PART 1

"I Feel Like I'm on a Roller Coaster"

chapter 1

Why You Get Stressed Out

For most people, there are many joys that go with being a teen. They may include hanging out with friends, losing yourself in a good TV show, catching the attention of that special guy or girl, and acing that school project that you never thought you'd make it through. How about when someone does something deliberately funny in class and you feel like you're going to burst from holding in your laughter? How about getting behind the wheel of a car for the first time and learning to drive?

As you already know from experience, however, being a teen isn't all sunshine and rainbows. The pressures and stress you face are no joke, and life can really feel like an uphill battle.

So, it might seem like one minute you're on top of the world, and the next minute you're in freefall. Being a teen, especially in today's fast-paced society, is like riding a roller coaster filled with steep climbs, insane drops, and tons of twists and turns. Which is why the demands, pressures, and anxieties you face can leave you feeling like you're holding on for dear life while the scenery whizzes past you. Sometimes it may seem that the heart-pounding ride will never let up, even though you desperately want relief from the white-knuckle, stomach-turning thrills. No wonder you occasionally lose it or freak out! Luckily, this book can teach you powerful and proven ways of slowing down your roller coaster.

Sadly, stress often has a very negative impact on teens. Being under constant pressure to succeed, to do well, or to be popular—whether you're pressuring yourself or feel pressured by others—can have unhealthy outcomes (see chapter 2). On the other hand, keep in mind that, as avid hikers say, "The best view comes after the hardest climb." This means that once you learn how to manage the stressors in your life, you'll be able to see challenges and demands more clearly and feel good about handling them well. You'll start to feel pride in your ability to attain positive outcomes even when things get tough.

What Is Stress?

There are many ways to define it, but "stress" usually refers to feeling overwhelmed by a difficult situation, by super-tough commitments, or by pressure from every direction. Some kinds of stress make you feel swamped; others make you feel squeezed. You may be familiar with a feeling of anxiety, frustration, sadness, or tiredness that arises when you're stressed out. Sadly, many teens who experience stress in this way think they're alone. But the truth is that a lot of teens struggle with difficult emotions triggered by stressful demands.

Some teens are more aware of the physical reactions and sensations, as opposed to the emotions, that stress can produce. They may frequently experience headaches, stomachaches, or other physical symptoms of being under pressure. These bodily reactions we'll describe in chapter 2 can serve as warning signs and signals to let you know when things are really getting to you.

Stress can affect us in varying other ways too. Do you often feel exhausted and emotionally and/or physically run down? Maybe stress has the opposite effect and makes you feel really alert and energized. Maybe it makes you want to vent about what's bothering you, or maybe it makes you want to shut everyone out. Whether you tend to feel wiped out or pace all around, or whether you confide in others or keep to yourself, just know that there are many ways that stress can impact you.

It's also important to realize that stress can come at you with varied intensity and duration. You may find that some days, or even entire weeks, go relatively smoothly and you hardly feel stressed out. On the other hand, some days you'd rather stay in bed and watch your favorite shows than deal with everything going on in your world!

What I'm trying to say is that no matter how you experience stress, it's a big-time challenge for most teens. A study conducted by the American Psychological Association (Bethune, 2014) found that on average, teens' stress levels rival those of adults. And during the school year, they're even higher.

The good news is that there are quick and easy strategies you can learn to help you manage your stress. Once you start using them, you'll be less weighed down, you'll focus better on your schoolwork and other activities, and you'll feel happier!

Spotting Stress

Being a teen in today's fast-moving world means that you're facing more demands on your time, and more stress, than you probably even realize. Right now, you might be dealing with any or all of the following frustrations, pressures, and worries.

*   Feeling seriously squeezed on time between school, after-school activities, your part-time job, and hanging out with friends

* Pressure to get good grades

* Getting teased (even if it's followed by "just kidding"), put down, or otherwise bullied

* Having peers actively or passively pulling away from you because you don't fit into the "popular group"

* Feeling like an outsider because of your personal interests, sexual orientation, racial identity, religion, or gender identity

* The ups and downs of real-life social connections or social media

* Feeling awkward in front of other, when you wish you could look "cool" and easygoing instead

You can really feel it when stressors are coming hard and fast. I'd be willing to bet that there are times when you know exactly what one of the following teens is talking about. Or maybe you're loaded down with such a jumbo-sized variety pack of pressures that you can relate to all of these statements all the time.

In Their Own Words

"Every time I tell my parents that I'm stressed out, they tell me that it's because I procrastinate doing my homework. That just makes me feel even more stressed out!"
Becky, age 14

"Everyone else is so great, and I'm only just me."
Shanice, age 15

"My coach keeps pushing me, and my dad says the same kinda crap all the time, thinking he's just helping me. Going to practice is never fun anymore. It's actually starting to suck."
Kurt, age 17

"I'm worried, frustrated, and pissed off all at the same time."
Tai, age 19

"It's just, like, I can't breathe when there is so much coming at me!" **Gary, age 13**

"Sometimes it's like everything gets piled on top of me, and if one thing slips, *everything* will fall." **Donny, age 15**

These teens were able to explain what stress is like for them, but often people don't realize how much they're stressed, or what exactly is stressing them out, if they haven't learned the many different ways that stress can manifest. Just know that all the following words describe emotional states that may be connected to stress. This can help you identify and start thinking and talking about your own stress.

Lousy	Tired	Aggravated
Angry	Fed up	Tense
Nervous	Burned out	Hopeless
Worried	Sad	Disappointed
Bored	Conflicted	Pissed off
Exhausted	Embarrassed	Upset
Overwhelmed	Mad	Sick of it
Freaking out	Overloaded	Numb

Corey struggled with some of the stressors mentioned above when he was moving from middle school to high school.

Corey's Story

After he finished eighth grade, Corey was really looking forward to high-school freedoms. As the summer ended, though, he felt nervous about being around more kids, being in larger classes, and having to make more decisions about which classes to take than in middle school. Plus, once he got to high school, he was suddenly aware that he was a bit overweight and not as muscular as many of the other boys.

The stress Corey felt from seeing himself as physically inferior to other kids fueled his social anxieties. It seemed like everyone else acted and talked so smooth, whereas he didn't feel confident at all. Corey dealt with his self-consciousness by mostly keeping to himself and clamming up. One of the boys he had hung out with in middle school told Corey that he needed to start dressing cooler, lifting weights, and partying, or else other kids would think he was a "head case." Between all the negative thoughts about not measuring up, and the grind of his classwork, Corey felt quite stressed out.

Your Brain's Stress-Detection and Response System

To really understand how stress impacts you, first you need to grasp how your brain detects and reacts to it. Learning the roles that different parts of your brain play in perceiving stress will prepare you to cope with it.

Your brain has a super-cool stress-response system that detects potential threats. This naturally developed *threat-response* system kicks into high gear whenever you're in a stressful situation. And it can happen in a matter of seconds.

The part of your brain that initially detects a threat is called the *amygdala*. This little structure deep inside your brain is something that all mammals have. The amygdala is what triggers basic emotions such as fear, anger, and sadness. It detects when you are physically in danger—for example, when you're frightened by a barking dog. Your amygdala notices these stressful threats by processing messages from your senses, the organs in your body, and your memory of past upsetting experiences (such as feeling afraid of dogs because one bit you in the past).

When your amygdala detects a threat, it signals another region of your brain called the *hypothalamus*, which wakes up your *pituitary gland*. Your hypothalamus is located in the center of your brain and plays a big role in stimulating hormone production, governing your body temperature, balancing out other important functions such as hunger and thirst, and regulating your emotions. The pituitary gland is attached to your hypothalamus. Your pituitary gland is referred to as the master gland, because it has a wide-ranging role in controlling many organs and processes in your body. Together, these parts of your brain compose the *limbic system*. When your limbic system perceives a threat, it stimulates the release of a hormone called *cortisol*.

Cortisol releases a flood of *glucose*, better known as *blood sugar*, into the bloodstream. This gives your body a high-octane injection. Another primitive part of your brain, the *hindbrain* (at the back of your head, near the base of your skull), works together with the limbic system (they're jointly referred to as the *reacting brain*). At the same time your limbic system is giving you a burst of fuel, your hindbrain—which controls your heart rate, your breathing, and the flow of blood to your limbs and organs—revs up your engines. You know your stress response is in full swing when you feel your heart thumping, your chest heaving, and your legs and arms tingling (from the increased blood flow).

Now your body is ready to use lots of energy, and fast, because if you don't do *something*, you're going to get hurt—at least, that's the assumption of your reacting brain. When you detect a threat, such as when you're startled by a barking dog, your brain doesn't bother to try to determine the precise extent and size of the threat. That's because it reckons there may not be time to *think*. Assessing all the variables—Is the dog on a leash? Is there a fence between you and the dog? How high is the fence? Could the dog jump over it or not?— might cost precious seconds as the dog leaps for your throat. Because of your self-preservation instinct, your brain takes a "better safe than sorry" approach and prepares you for a life-or-death struggle. For the moment, you're ready to do whatever may be necessary to survive. This is your body's *fight, flight, or freeze* response, the same response that enabled your ancient ancestors to take immediate and decisive action—to attack, to run away, or to play dead—when encountering a scary beast, such as a saber-toothed tiger.

In most animals, the threat-detection system of the brain responds to physical dangers. In modern humans, it also perceives situations that are only *emotionally* scary. So it reacts to fears you may have about a test or an assignment, an audition for the school play, or a tryout for the cheerleading squad. This can become a problem, because the fight, flight, or freeze response is total overkill for dealing with the common stresses of being a teen. For example, if your teacher gives you a tough assignment and you feel threatened—thinking, *There's no way I can do that!*—it won't do you any good to hurl a book at the teacher (fight), or run out of the classroom (take flight), or say nothing and not move (freeze, hoping the teacher will think you're dead and leave you alone).

Nevertheless, your heart races and you start to hyperventilate. It might be the same story when you're facing a tight project deadline, coming face to face with someone who spread gossip about you, trying to get good grades in school, feeling buried under responsibilities, dealing with people who annoy you, or trying to keep your act together when people are judging you. Your body is gearing up to react big-time, putting unnecessary strain on your system.

Since it wouldn't be helpful or even socially acceptable to act on your primitive survival impulses whenever you're in an uncomfortable situation, sometimes you just bottle them up. Then, later, you explode (or implode). For example, you might hold in your rage all day long and then yell at someone or throw something (satisfying your urge to fight). Or, you may start feeling super-worried or sad but keep these emotions locked up while shutting yourself off to other people (satisfying your urge to freeze). When you hold in your anger or fear instead of letting it out, it's like you're emotionally constipated. Over time, this can lead to:

* Depression

* Anxiety

* Weight gain

* Acne

* Fatigue

* Increased risk of addictions

* Physical health problems (e.g., headaches, stomach issues, and other aches or pains)

The good news is that you can manage how you respond to stressful events in your life. You don't have to let your emotions rule your behavior, but you don't have to stuff them down either. Thanks to the part of your brain that helps you think through and challenge emotional thoughts, you can learn to interpret and react to difficult and demanding situations in more reasonable ways. This logical part of your brain can help you feel more in charge when your stress is getting out of hand.

Your Reacting Brain Can Be Tamed by Your Thinking Brain

While in modern life you thankfully don't meet any saber-toothed tigers, everyday challenges can still make you want to scream—thanks to your old-school reacting brain. Fortunately, you can learn to bring another part of your brain, called the prefrontal cortex (the "thinking" part), online. The main job of the prefrontal cortex is to provide logical thinking to help control your emotional responses to stress so that you don't get too stressed out and overreact.

Place your finger on your forehead, and you'll be about as close as you can get to touching your prefrontal cortex. Your prefrontal cortex can rein in your stress response, slowing down the release of cortisol—*if* it determines that whatever your amygdala is freaking out about is not in fact a threat or if it recognizes that the situation is manageable.

This logical thinking part of your brain, your prefrontal cortex, is very important for helping you not to overreact and helping you make good choices. And as you'll see, often when you feel stressed out, you have to consciously remember to turn to your thinking brain to gain back control from your reacting brain.

It'll be helpful to begin each activity in this book by taking a few deep breaths. This is because mindfully focusing on your breath (or doing something like counting to ten) helps direct your awareness away from the rapid-fire thoughts being generated by your reacting brain, clearing the way to engage your prefrontal cortex. Going back to the example of the barking dog, this ability to calm yourself down and assess the risk of the situation with your thinking brain helps you evaluate whether the dog presents a threat to you.

Even as a teen, you can learn to train your thinking brain to see situations that stress you out as less overwhelming and stressful. In fact, this is a great time for you to strengthen that brain "muscle," because it's still growing. Most people's prefrontal cortex doesn't reach its full size until they're in their mid-twenties. How cool is that? Your body may not have matured as early as you hoped for, if you're like Corey, but if you use your thinking brain to control and guide your reacting brain, you can get a well-developed prefrontal cortex. What's more, it'll be your good friend—always there to talk you down in a crisis and help you make the right decisions.

Right now, your life is full of opportunities to use your thinking brain to help you calm down in stressful situations. Just think about the kinds of things that happen again and again if you're like most teens:

* You forgot to start writing a paper, and it's due tomorrow.

* You thought it would be cool to audition for the school play, but now you're really nervous about going through with it.

* The person you're dating is acting differently toward you, and you're worried that they'll break up with you.

* A friend you thought you could count on is now dating your ex-boyfriend.

* You feel anxious about asking someone out.

* You have to tell your parents something they won't be too happy about.

The last time you were facing a situation like this, how stressed out did you feel? What happened in the end? Was it really as bad as you thought it would be? Was it worth the fear and panic? Do you wish you had been able to think about things differently?

When you step back for a moment, just how large is the role that stress plays in your life? You may be surprised. The following activity can help you get a sense of the big picture.

Try This! Picturing Your Roller Coaster

Find a quiet place to sit and reflect for a few minutes about the stressors you've experienced so far as a teen. Try to remember, in as much detail as you can, a difficult situation related to school, your peers, your family, a sport, another activity, or a part-time job. Consider the things that people were saying, who else was there, the demands and pressures you were under, and how you felt in that moment. The following questions can help you become more aware of how stressful events like this one affect your daily life.

How often do you feel stressed out?

How does being stressed out negatively impact you?

Does your stress negatively impact those around you? If so, how?

How do you generally respond to stressful situations?

If you could go back in time, what's one stressful situation you wish you could've handled better?

What past stressful situations have you overcome, or at least managed? How did it feel when you were able to do this?

Do you ever talk about your stress, or do you keep it to yourself?

Putting It All Together

In this chapter, you began to think about what stress means for you. We compared the stress of teenage life to being on a roller-coaster ride. You learned about how your brain works to detect and respond to things that scare you, and how, although this ability helped your ancestors, it's not a great match for modern life. But simply bottling up those big emotions generated by your reacting brain has negative effects sooner or later. The prefrontal cortex is the "thinking" part of the brain that can intervene and help you find a "middle road." We ended this chapter by having you look at how stress impacts you personally, to get you thinking about how your life could feel less frantic if you only knew how to start managing your stress.

In the next chapter, we'll take a look at how a human body (yes, even yours) lets its owner know when it's feeling stressed out. As you'll see, listening to your body's stress signals can help you realize when it's time to use your new brake levers on your roller-coaster ride.

chapter 2

Noticing Your Body's Stress Signals

Want to guess what roller coasters and human bodies have in common? The answer is that they both suffer a lot wear and tear due to stress. Have you ever been on an old wooden roller coaster, one that was making all kinds of creaking and rattling noises? If so, you might have worried that something would break. Instead of screaming with fright at how fast you were going, you were probably groaning from the beating your body was taking as you juddered around the track. Maybe your head started to pound because it kept banging against the back of the seat, and your recent lunch threatened to make a reappearance. Yuck! Kind of like that, stress that's left unmanaged can lead to headaches and stomach issues, among other physical ailments.

Maybe you're the kind of person who doesn't show it when you're feeling stressed. For example, you don't cuss and slam doors when you're pissed off, or you don't burst into tears when someone ruins your day. Scientists have known for a long time, though, that the stress we keep inside still affects our bodies. William Osler, an eighteenth-century physician, figured out that negative emotions that went unexpressed could lead to internal health issues. As he put it, "The organs weep the tears the eyes refuse to shed." This timeless wisdom suggests that our bodies react big-time to the stressful feelings we experience in our daily lives.

As a teen, you've got a long life ahead of you. So it's important to get in the habit of listening to your body and paying attention to any parts that are trying to let you know there may be some problems. Taking time to keep everything working smoothly behind the scenes may help you avoid problems that can force you to close down for repairs. So tend to those squeaks and rattles before you really come unglued.

Some common physical consequences of stress that can put you "out of order" are:

* Colds

* Viral infections

* Migraine headaches

* Eating disorders

* Asthma

* Skin conditions

* Gastrointestinal concerns, such as irritable bowel syndrome

In this chapter first you'll get an appreciation of how stress in your mind shows up in your body so that you can avoid outcomes like these by knowing when to use your CBT and positive psychology brake levers (which you'll learn about later) to keep your roller coaster of stress from running out of control. Then you can explore some ways to reduce the tension in your body to help lower the stress in your mind, even if you're not currently experiencing physical symptoms of stress.

Hormones Bridge Your Mind and Body

In chapter 1, we discussed your brain's threat-response system. To recap, when your brain perceives something stressful, your hormones quickly release stored glucose to increase your body's energy. And your adrenal glands inject the hormones adrenaline and cortisol into your bloodstream to amp you up. This results in the fight, flight, or freeze response. As we discussed earlier, while this really cool survival mechanism has kept our human species alive, the everyday sources of stress that we encounter don't merit the full stress response with which our minds race and our bodies reflexively tense up.

Intense Emotions and Bodily Tension

For teens, emotions can feel super-intense. That's because stress-related hormones kick in much more quickly and are harder to rein in for teens than they are for adults. Remember, the part of your brain that assesses danger, reasons things out, and can call off the stress response (the fight, flight, or freeze response)—your prefrontal cortex (the thinking part of your brain)—isn't fully developed. Hey, don't feel bad, because it's also true that the way your teen brain is wired helps you learn many things better than adults can! You'll see how this will work to your advantage for learning the stress-lowering CBT and positive psychology skills we'll talk about later.

We all have a mind-body connection, and that's why strong emotions create sensations in your body. When you're feeling nervous about things like school, peer pressure, issues at home, or that special person you *really* like—especially if you're tired or someone pushes your buttons—your roller coaster may feel like it's doing loops! When this happens, your hormones kick in, and your thinking brain loses the ability to control your bodily reactions.

The key point to remember is that when facing frequent and/ or intense daily uncertainties and pressures related to school, social situations, or relationships—or, for that matter, any kind of stressful demands—your body responds by involuntarily tensing up. And this tension can last for days or weeks. This is your body's way of saying to you, "Hey it's getting really tense in here, and you need to do some calming activities or else you might flip out." Give the next activity a try to learn more about how your body may be signaling to you that you're stressed out.

Try This! Discovering Your Personal Stress Signals

Have you ever noticed how your body reacts when you experience stress? Bodily tension can manifest in various ways, not just as tightness in your muscles. Here are some physical symptoms that people commonly experience when they feel stressed out.

- Rapid breathing
- Headache
- Queasiness (butterflies in the stomach)
- Back or neck ache
- Dry mouth
- Sudden exhaustion
- Chronic tiredness
- Stomachache
- Sweaty palms
- Flushed or hot cheeks
- Fast heartbeat
- Feeling tired
- Inability to concentrate
- Feeling weak
- Trembling
- Loss of appetite
- Sleep problems
- Cramps

Which of the above physical symptoms do you tend to feel when stress is impacting you?

Do you ever notice these symptoms happening together or in a certain order (for example, you feel tired and then you start getting a headache or tightness or pain somewhere else)?

When do you experience these symptoms most often? What stressful situations do you think they might relate to?

How can being on the lookout for bodily symptoms help you manage future stressors that come your way?

Here are some representative quotes from teens about the ways in which their bodies reflect the stress going on in their mind.

In Their Own Words

"I thought I was going to throw up when I had to meet my dad's new girlfriend. It's just so totally weird to see him with someone else. It was seriously disgusting, too, because they were, like, all over each other." **Asha, age 14**

"I was super stressed out when I sat down to take that test. My hands were shaking, and my head was pounding. I was scared I was going to fail." **Barry, age 15**

"When I get really stressed out, I get super-impatient and snappy with people on the outside, but inside I feel like I'm gonna blow up from feeling so much pressure!"
Barbara, age 16

"I've been so stressed out and worried, now I'm totally exhausted." **Chet, age 17**

"I get totally bloated after I eat when I'm stressed out. A doctor told me it's called 'irritable bowel syndrome.' Ugh!"
Julie, age 18

The Mind-Body Stress Reaction Cycle

One reason it's important to be on the lookout for aches, pains, and other physical symptoms of stress is so that when you get them, you don't think, *What the heck is wrong with me?!* If that happens, you might become concerned or even begin to panic, thinking you're ill or having a medical emergency. Noticeable symptoms of anxiety, such as excessive sweating, can understandably make you self-conscious, piling on to your stress. If you don't connect the way you're feeling to what's happening in your life, your stress can get worse by feeding on your worried thoughts and physical reactions, as shown in the following diagram.

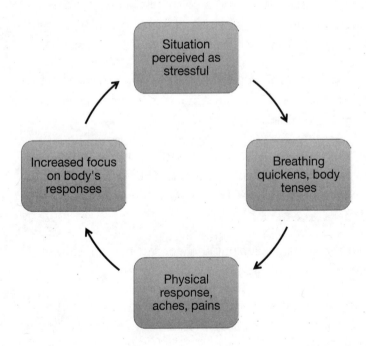

When you begin to tune in to your body's stress signals, your physical symptoms will feel much less scary, because you'll recognize them as a normal automatic response to hassles and burdens. Learning to tune in to your body's stress signals is, thus, extra helpful for managing stress! For example, one sixteen-year-old said that before she learned to monitor herself for physical symptoms of stress, she didn't know why some days she suffered from pounding headaches. Once she started to notice that her headaches usually come on after she had stayed up way too late the previous night to finish a project for school, not only did she stop worrying why her head hurt, but she was able to target the problem of waiting until the last minute to do her schoolwork so that she got headaches less often.

The key is to *really* listen to how and when your body gives you stress-related messages. By listening to your body in this way, you'll know to take action and cope with your stress instead of just letting it wear on you physically and emotionally!

When you can pay closer attention to stress-related body signals such as fatigue, upset stomach, headaches, and muscle tension, you can start to take better care of yourself, calm yourself down, and prevent yourself from becoming further stressed out when your roller coaster is already zooming.

Here's what happened when Lora was obsessing about stress in her mind that was coming out in her body.

Lora's Story

Lora was having a really stressful year in school. For one thing, the group of girls she hung out with had changed in ways she didn't much like. Compared with last year, now they were way too much about drama and competing for attention from boys. Some of them had started smoking weed. She tried it a couple of times, and it made her feel really out of it. As time went on, Lora realized that she didn't want to smoke weed, nor did she want to pretend that she did in an effort to keep her friends who seemed to like it. For another thing, her classes had gotten a lot harder.

It all really hit Lora when midterms came around and her right arm, from her hand all the way up to her shoulder, got super-tight. Of course, telling herself over and over that she was going to fail her tests made her feel like she was even "gripping harder" on that stress roller coaster, which was soaring around faster than ever. After a few more months, her shoulder pain got really bad. When she looked up her symptoms on a popular medical website, they seemed to point to a ton of frightening health issues. This stressed her out so much that she begged her parents to take her to a doctor.

The doctor told Lora it was probably muscle tension due to stress, but Lora wasn't convinced. Pain like this can't just be a symptom of being under too much pressure, *she thought.* I'm not that big a wuss! *It wasn't until Lora's parents took her to a psychologist that she discovered just how much she was making herself stressed out. She learned to pay attention to her body and relax, and her shoulder pain slowly improved.*

Note: See Your Health Care Provider If Your Physical Symptoms Get Worse Because experiencing stress through your body is a normal and common occurrence, try not to obsess about it as Lora did. But do let your parents or a responsible adult in your life know if you experience pain that comes on suddenly or lasts for more than a few days, so that you can be evaluated by a qualified health care professional as soon as possible. In some cases, stress-related symptoms are similar to ones that may signal more serious health concerns (for example, abdominal pain may indicate a ruptured appendix, which needs immediate attention).

Listening to Your Body for Taking Action

It's important to stay mindful that your body communicates not only to let you know you're stressed, but also to let you know when serious threats might be coming your way. If your chest starts pounding when you're about to get into a car with a driver who's high or drunk, your brain is warning you, and with good reason—you and the driver could get in an accident or wind up in trouble with the police. If you're walking in a crime-ridden area in the middle of the night, and your legs feel like they're ready to spring into a sprint, that nagging feeling can help you be alert to danger and stay safe. So, when you notice a stressful physical sensation, consider whether you're about to do some-thing that breaks a rule or could endanger your own or someone else's well-being. It may be helpful to ask yourself, *If my parents knew about this, what would they think?* If they would disapprove (for good reason), you'll probably want to remove yourself from the situation or take sen-sible precautions rather than try to convince yourself to relax.

A Few Simple Relaxation Strategies

Since your mind and body are connected, taking steps to directly address tension in your body by doing some simple relaxing exercises can not only relieve your symptoms but also lower your stress level.

As you do the next three activities, remember that muscle tension is the common denominator that lets you know when stress is in your body. By working directly with your body to reduce this muscle tension, you'll help your CBT and positive psychology brake levers work even better!

Any one of these exercises can help you smooth out a bumpy roller-coaster ride by focusing on what's holding it up—your muscles. The first involves just using your hand to get the immediate sense of controlling a certain part of your body. The second is a full-body rapid-relaxation exercise. The third is a brief body scan, which is a mindfulness exercise that helps you observe tension in your body in a neutral, nonjudgmental way, to help you let that tension go.

Try This! Squeezing an Imaginary Lemon

Imagine that there's a lemon in front of you. Take a moment to visualize it in as much detail as you can. Then, with your right hand, reach out into the air and pretend you're grabbing that lemon. Imagine its weight and the way it feels in your palm. Now picture there's a hole cut in the end of the lemon, and try to squeeze that lemon so that some juice comes out. Notice how your right hand and arm are tense as you grip and squeeze that lemon for five to seven seconds. Okay, now pretend to set the lemon back down, and feel your hand and arm relax. Repeat this three times, each time trying to squeeze even more juice out and then relaxing your arm.

How did it feel to squeeze the lemon?

Could you feel the difference between your arm muscles being tense and your arm muscles being relaxed?

Now that you're not holding the lemon any longer, does your arm feel more relaxed or more tense than when you started?

Can you see how focusing on your body in this way could help take your mind off of stressful thoughts for a while?

You can do this exercise as a quick tension reliever any time that stress is getting to you. Your imagination will supply you with as many lemons as you need.

Now let's have you do a rapid stress-reducing exercise that focuses on letting go of muscle tension in your whole body.

Try This! Rapid Full-Body Tension Reliever

Sit in a chair, or lie down in a comfortable position. Now quickly contract every muscle you can in your body and hold for ten seconds. Be sure to breathe as you do this exercise, and repeat it three times. Rest for about ten to fifteen seconds between each repetition.

Did you notice your body increasingly relaxing after each set of full muscle contractions?

Were the sensations of letting go of the tension in your entire body pleasant or unpleasant?

Does tensing and relaxing your entire body give you a better sense of the level of stress-related muscle tension you carry around on a daily basis?

Does rapidly tensing and relaxing your full body seem like an efficient way to manage stressful situations?

You can do the next exercise while lying down or sitting. The way it's presented here is for lying down. You may want to listen to the recording of this exercise available at http://www.newharbinger.com/43911. Another way to do it is to have someone read the steps aloud to you. Or, if you like, record yourself reading the steps and then follow along to the sound of your own voice.

Try This! Brief Body Scan

1. Lie down on a rug, a carpet, or another comfortable surface.

2. If you want to, you can close your eyes. Or leave them open as you do this exercise.

3. Gently bring your attention to the feeling of your body resting on the floor.

4. Take a few deep, relaxing breaths.

5. Focus your attention on your feet. You don't need to tense or relax them— just notice to what degree they feel tense or relaxed, or comfortable or uncomfortable, at this moment. Breathe in and out, and notice any sensations that are present or that come up in your feet. You don't need to evaluate these sensations or to try to change them in any way.

6. When you feel ready, gently shift your attention up your body to the next area, your lower legs. Spend a few moments focusing on what you feel there, just as you did for your feet.

7. Similarly, gently tune in to your knees. Then tune in to your upper legs.

8. Move your attention up your body. First focus on your buttocks and pelvis, then spend a while on your hands and arms, and then pay attention to your torso and back. End with your face and head.

9. Take a few more relaxing breaths. Whenever you're ready, open your eyes and slowly stand up.

    Which areas of your body seemed the loosest? Which ones were the most tense?

    How did it feel to simply observe the sensations in your body without reacting to them?

    Did spending some time just observing your body feel comfortable, or did it feel foreign or even strange?

    Was this exercise a pleasant activity?

    As a result of doing this exercise, did you feel the stress in your body increase or decrease?

Putting It All Together

In this chapter, we discussed how your body can sometimes give you trouble when you're stressed out. You learned about the stress-related connection between your body and your mind. Now that you have a better awareness of the signals your body tends to give you when you experience stress, when you notice these symptoms in the future you can repeat the relaxing exercises from this chapter to make your roller-coaster ride more comfortable. I recommend using the Bodily Symptoms Tracker worksheet, at http://www.newharbinger .com/43911, to help you stay aware of your physical reactions to stressful situations.

There may even be some times when just a few quick mindful breaths can kick-start your thinking brain after something stresses you out. Staying tuned in to your body can also help you know when it's time to pull your CBT and positive psychology brake levers. In the next chapter, we'll get into CBT by talking about some ways to slow down those thoughts and feelings that go racing through your mind, and some ways to cope, when you're stressed out.

chapter 3

Getting to Know the Brakes

The truth is that there is no actual stress or anxiety in the world; it's your thoughts that create these false beliefs.

This quotation is from Dr. Wayne Dyer, one of the best-known self-help experts of the late twentieth century. It may sound hard to believe, but it's true—as Dyer went on to point out, you can't see stress or touch it; you only have stressful thoughts. Fortunately, we can use our thinking brains to manage our stress instead of letting our reacting brains stress us out.

In this chapter, I'll introduce you to two types of brake levers for slowing down the racing thoughts and upset feelings that can accelerate your roller coaster. The first brake lever is taken from cognitive behavioral therapy (CBT). CBT is about consciously modifying (a) your thought process (your *cognition*) and (b) your behaviors to help you feel calmer when the going gets tough. The second brake lever comes from positive psychology. Positive psychology is about seeing your strengths, meeting challenges to feel good about yourself, gaining gratitude, and developing an optimistic outlook. This book combines the skills of CBT and positive psychology to provide you with a simple yet powerful combo—a one-two punch—for managing the stress in your life. CBT skills will be the subject of part 2 of this book, and positive psychology forms the basis of part 3.

What Is CBT?

CBT is a counseling approach that helps people identify the thoughts and beliefs (in this book, I often use the terms "thoughts" and "beliefs" interchangeably) that are upsetting them or stressing them out. This helps make big bumps on their roller coaster seem less scary or helps them handle events in their lives that they once found difficult. That's because a big part of *how* we experience certain events (at a very basic level, for example, whether an event is "good" or "bad") is influenced by *our thoughts* about them (Beck 2018). In other words, what we believe those events *mean*—about us, other people, the future, and so on—has a huge influence on how we feel about them.

Having negative thoughts about a difficult situation is normal. No one can stay positive all the time. And you can't force yourself to stop having unhelpful, upsetting thoughts. But if you let your reacting brain fuel those thoughts, they can spiral out of control. This can lead you to assume that the situation is hopeless or you're headed for disaster. As a result, you may do things that don't really help, which can ultimately become destructive patterns in your life or leave you unhappy.

You can, however, train your thinking brain to have stronger helpful thoughts, to counter your reacting brain's upsetting and unhelpful thoughts! Your helpful thoughts about situations can lead you to better feelings and better outcomes.

The Cycle of Thoughts, Feelings, and Actions

The thoughts we have influence the feelings we have, and the feelings we have influence what we do next. Then, what we did next influences the thoughts we have later, and so on. The following diagram illustrates how negative thoughts, feelings, and actions occur in a cyclical manner.

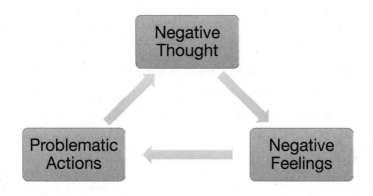

As you can see from the diagram, according to the CBT model, negative thoughts drive negative feelings, which lead to problematic behaviors. If you don't interrupt the cycle, you can get locked into a spiral of doom and gloom. Let's look at how stress, if you don't manage it well, can keep your roller coaster going in circles or send you down a dead end path. Here are some examples of ways that teens may manage their stress that don't turn out so well. If you've done some of these things too, don't feel bad—we're all human, and stress gets the better of everyone sometimes.

Letting Stress Slip into Anger

This problem is actually very common. When they feel stressed, many teens become confrontational. For example, they say mean things in anger. Others tend to be passive-aggressive—for example, punishing their family members by giving them the silent treatment. Anger can lead to all sorts of unexpected and unfriendly behaviors. Some teens even misunderstand their anger as a signal that they "have to hit or throw something."

As mentioned in chapter 1, while bottling up your stress may work to get you through the day, it usually leads to anger and other problems. One thing I can tell you for sure is that no teen has ever reported to me that punching holes in walls is a healthier way to manage stress-related anger than the ones you'll learn in this book!

Withdrawing and Avoiding Behaviors

As a teen, you very likely just want to feel normal and not stressed out. Sometimes it may feel tempting to turn away from your demands and responsibilities as a way to get away from the feelings of stress. But this can rob you of valuable opportunities or other ways to help yourself. For example, if you tend to feel uncomfortable in social situations and avoid starting a conversation with someone you like at school because it makes you feel queasy, then you won't get to know anyone. Furthermore, to continue this example, if you haven't looked at the physical symptoms of stress (chapter 2), you might not realize that the reason you're queasy each Monday morning is because you're so nervous about your crush. In that case, you might assume that you're sick and should stay home from school. Missing school, of course, leads to its own problems. If you tend to miss a lot of school or other activities due to the physical symptoms listed in chapter 2, you may be mismanaging your stress.

Overeating or Undereating

One unfortunately common way that people cope with stress-related feelings is by *emotional eating*, or trying to soothe their negative emotions with food. Have you ever eaten just to take your mind off what's bothering you—perhaps when you were really anxious, sad, lonely, or bored? Or maybe you have the opposite problem, where you lose your appetite whenever you feel really stressed out.

For persistent or worsening issues having to do with eating or not eating, please ask your parents or another caring adult about the possibility of seeing a qualified mental health professional.

Using Drugs or Alcohol/Self-Harm/ Reckless Behaviors

Sadly, many teens (and adults) turn to unhealthy ways to manage worries. Maybe you or people you know have tried drinking alcohol or smoking marijuana and using other drugs to escape the feeling of being stressed out. Drug use is frequently connected to underlying stress related to worries or boredom. Whether seemingly innocent curiosity leads you to experiment with drugs, or you use them to alleviate sadness, anxiety, or frustration, they may lead to more problems including harming your body and creating addictions.

Engaging in self-harming behaviors, such as cutting, is another unhealthy way of escaping your worries that can also harm your body. If you or someone you know feels suicidal, talk to a qualified mental health professional right away or call the National Suicide Prevention Life Line at 1-800-273-8255.

Excessive Screen Time

Using screen time as an escape from worries may not seem like a big deal when compared with other negative behaviors you could engage in. Yet it can really become a problem if digital distractions keep you from meeting demands and facing pressures in your life.

Do you have trouble setting or sticking to reasonable time limits on your screen usage? Do you often binge-watch shows without meaning to, or let one level of a video game suck you into another...and another?

An important consideration in determining whether your screen time is having a negative impact is to look at whether you're involved in other activities too. Do you participate in sports, the arts, or clubs at school? Do you have a part-time job? Or do you spend too many hours in front of a screen to do these things? In addition, is your screen time interfering with your ability to get enough sleep?

How Can CBT Skills Help?

As you've probably figured out, coping with stress by engaging in any of the above unhealthy behavior patterns is only going to make you feel worse in the end.

For example, let's say you recently changed schools, and you're looking for a place to sit in the cafeteria at lunchtime. You spot a girl you've said hi to in the hallways, but she's sitting with a group of people you've never met. You think *I'd like to go sit at that table, but they'll probably reject me*, which makes you anxious and discouraged. As a result, you choose to sit at an empty table (withdrawing/avoiding behavior), letting this chance to connect with a potential group of friends pass you by (and ensuring that you remain lonely yet another day).

CBT skills can help you identify, challenge, and replace your unhelpful or counterproductive thoughts, feelings, and actions. In the cafeteria example, you could reframe the situation and try thinking about things differently. In response to the thought *They'll probably reject me*, you could argue, *They seem cool, and I do kind of know a few of them*. That might help you feel more confident to go to their table, and you'll likely feel really good about yourself for taking this important step to expand your friend group.

For another example, imagine that you arrive in your first-period classroom and sit down as usual. Then the teacher announces it's time to discuss the assignment that you forgot to submit last night through the school online portal. You feel your face turning red. You beat yourself up over this embarrassing situation with thoughts like *I suck at life! I just can't manage anything right!* You shut down and decide to not do the assignment, even though you're still responsible for completing it. As a result, you'll receive a zero, and you might get a poor grade in the class, which won't sit well with you or your parents. Now imagine that, instead, you look at the situation in a less self-critical way and say to yourself: *Everyone makes mistakes. Yes, I am frustrated right now, but I'll discuss this with my teacher and work hard and quickly to make this assignment up.*

As you can see, by using CBT skills when you feel stressed out, you can learn to identify the counterproductive thoughts that pop up in your mind, evaluate them, and respond to them. Once you practice generating better, healthier thoughts, you'll be in a great position to manage stress and to be more successful when facing challenges.

In the examples above, it was assumed that you knew exactly what was stressing you out. But at other times, you might be feeling anxious, stressed, sad, or angry for no reason in particular. This is actually quite normal for teens! What's great about CBT skills is that you don't have to try to figure out what happened or who's to blame. You can start to actively reduce your stress level instead of feeling like a helpless victim of stress. CBT skills can put *you* in charge of your thoughts, feelings, and behaviors!

CBT Uses Your Thinking Brain to Calm Your Reacting Brain

Our amygdala-driven reacting brains can lead us to blindly follow our emotions. As illustrated by the examples above, your racing thoughts and upsetting emotions can lead you astray when dealing with difficult situations.

Let's take a closer look at how CBT skills work by seeing how Cassandra dealt with a brief, awkward, upsetting social situation. We'll also look at how she found a more helpful, positive way to view and cope with the situation.

Cassandra's Story

While Cassandra was walking through the school hallway, her new friend, Tamika, passed her by without acknowledging her. Cassandra took it personally, and her emotional roller coaster suddenly lurched forward. Cassandra thought: She just dissed me! I can never keep any friends. *Cassandra's accelerating thoughts led her to feel sad, empty, and rejected. As a way to cope with these feelings, Cassandra chose to ignore Tamika when she saw her later on, because deep down she was scared of being further hurt and rejected by her.*

Then Cassandra took some time to reevaluate the situation. She reflected on Tamika's having ignored her in the hallway: Wow, that was strange—but wait a minute, that's not like Tamika to just ignore someone with no explanation. *This thought made her wonder whether something was up with her friend, and she decided,* I'll try to catch her tomorrow and make sure she's doing okay. *The next day, she texted Tamika after school to see if they could get together for a minute before homeroom period the next morning. Cassandra wanted to check in with Tamika, due to her unusual behavior, in case she was going through a rough time and could use some help. Sure enough, when they met up, Tamika burst into tears and told Cassandra that a guy she liked was now dating another girl. In other words, when Tamika had seemingly snubbed Cassandra, it was because she was totally preoccupied with feeling rejected and had never even noticed Cassandra. And when Cassandra reached out to Tamika, she and Tamika became closer, rather than growing apart.*

Can you see how two very different ways of thinking about the same situation can generate different feelings and possibly different outcomes?

Now let's consider another stressful situation, this time with Steve, whose negative, rigid thinking really got in his way for coping with a science test.

Steve's Story

At the end of science class on Friday, Steve's teacher reminded everyone about an important test coming up on Monday. Steve, who hadn't been keeping up well lately, started to think, I'm going to fail this test. *Steve's stress-response system then further reacted to this thought with a flood of worries.* Not only am I going to fail this test, but I'll probably now fail the class for the year. *This led to an even worse thought:* I'm doomed! *Sadly, he kept his thoughts and feelings to himself.*

Steve desperately wanted to avoid these overpowering thoughts and feelings about failing this big test. He tried to escape his stress by playing video games and spending a lot of time on social media. Yet these distracting activities added to his stress, because they made him feel isolated. Even worse, he didn't think it would be acceptable to talk to anyone about his racing, worried thoughts. He didn't want to appear weak and vulnerable to his friends. Sadly, Steve retreated further into playing even more video games, which grew increasingly appealing as an escape from all the worries.

By avoiding his schoolwork and test preparation, Steve let his roller coaster of stress take him on a wild ride. His unchallenged negative self-talk led him to feel anxiety, which he unfortunately chose to bottle up. Steve's avoidance through playing video games then left his worry and anxiety unresolved and *ended up making the situation worse, because the test was still going to happen and he wouldn't be prepared at all.*

Fortunately, Steve's mom noticed that something was up. She arranged for Steve to meet with his school counselor. As discussed below, Steve learned some valuable CBT skills from his school counselor to help him manage his negative self-talk and avoidance of important school responsibilities.

Tackling Counterproductive Thoughts

CBT helps you look at your thoughts that are unrealistic and sometimes harsh and learn to challenge and replace them with more realistic and supportive thoughts. So when Steve noticed thoughts about failing, he challenged the thought *I'm going to fail* with the more helpful thought *This test won't be easy, but I'll definitely do better if I try to study for it.*

This process of reevaluating and challenging problematic thoughts, which is the essence of CBT, is sometimes referred to as *cognitive restructuring*. CBT teaches us that just because we *have* a thought doesn't mean that it's true. This is super-important for managing stress, because the thoughts that trouble us and stress us out tend to misrepresent the facts. Yet we allow them to guide our decisions. Sometimes, we believe a thought simply because it's one we've had so often; other times, because it's easy; other times, because it fits with our preexisting beliefs. The truth is that many of the negative things you tell yourself contain one or more *cognitive distortions* (think of them as mutated thoughts). Like a funhouse mirror, rather than reflecting the world as it is, cognitive distortions warp and twist the image, making it seem ugly or even frightening. They include (Grohol 2019):

* **All-or-nothing thinking:** If something in your life isn't perfect, then everything is a mess. So, for example, if you don't get an A on that test, then you (unfairly!) see yourself as a total failure. This is otherwise known as *polarized thinking.*

* **Jumping to conclusions:** You reckon you know what's on someone else's mind or can predict how people will act. As an example, you're sure that no one will talk to you if you go to the party this weekend, because everyone there will be judging you.

* **Negative filtering:** You focus on the negative aspects of a situation and exaggerate or magnify them, while failing

to see any positives. For example, your teacher says you did a nice job on your oral presentation but gave you one piece of constructive feedback: next time, you might talk a little more slowly. Now all you can think about is how you talked too quickly, and you feel disappointed in yourself, when instead you could be feeling good about the praise you received overall.

* **Catastrophizing:** You expect the worst possible things to happen. These thoughts usually start with "What if?" For example: *What if I don't make the baseball team, and kids give me crap about it for the rest of the year?* This is also known as "magnifying" or "minimizing."

* **"Should" thinking:** You have a list of rigid rules about how you and others should behave. Let's say you're frustrated about how long it's taking you to do a single math problem. You wonder angrily: *What's wrong with me? This math problem shouldn't be so hard to do.*

Sometimes teens, and even adults, think that beating themselves up with the word "should" makes them feel or look noble. The reality is that it leads to shame. And shame can sap your motivation to get things done and reach your goals.

* **Labeling:** You stick a negative label on yourself. Frequent labels that teens unfairly saddle themselves with when it comes to schoolwork are "lazy" and "stupid."

* **Negative comparisons:** You unfavorably compare yourself to others. Other people's lives are great, and they have it all together, whereas something about you doesn't measure up. You may be comparing yourself to people in the media

or the people you sit next to every day. For example, you think, *She's thinner and she's prettier than I am.* Or *He's a star athlete, and hot girls like him; who cares if people think I'm smart? I'm still jealous.*

Some psychology experts use the term *ANTs* (*automatic negative thoughts*) instead of *cognitive distortions.* Whether you want to think of them as ANTs, cognitive distortions, counterproductive thoughts, or something else (for the most part in this book, we'll call them "distorted negative thoughts"), it's important to realize that these troublesome thoughts are usually inaccurate, inflexible, overly pessimistic, or exaggerated. The main point is that there are more reasonable ways to view your challenges and struggles. The next activity will give you an introduction to battling distorted thoughts you may have about school. Then, in chapter 4, you'll learn how to develop the following skills so that you can practice using them in a variety of situations:

* Identifying your unhelpful thoughts

* Questioning these beliefs to see if they are, in fact, true

* Replacing your distorted negative thoughts with more positive ones

* Visualizing and carrying out emotionally healthier behaviors and making better choices in certain situations

CBT skills do take some practice, because we typically are so used to letting our automatic self-talk fly under the radar.

Once you go through the activity below, you'll likely emerge with a better awareness of how distorted negative thoughts fire up your stress level. Learning to identify these unhelpful thoughts will give you the ability to question and challenge them so that you can stop them from getting in the way of your living an easier and happier life

Try This! Exploring Your Unhelpful Thoughts

Just because your reacting brain leads you to doubt your abilities, that doesn't mean that you have to buy into these stressful thoughts. For example, think about the most frequent struggles that you have in school (we'll discuss school stress in greater detail in chapter 8). Do tests, presentations, and homework demands trigger especially bad worries? On a piece of paper, draw three columns.

Label the first column "Negative Thoughts About School," and write down three to five negative thoughts you had recently or typically have on this subject. Think of something specific that made you feel bad, and include that in the thought. For example, "Mr. Jones is way too strict, and he makes school totally suck!" Sometimes it can be hard to get at the thoughts that are really underlying your stress about school (or any other area of your life). Just try to identify any rigid thoughts that feel upsetting.

For the second column, label it "Helpful Thoughts" and write down a more helpful thought to go with each one you wrote in the first column. Try to put things in perspective or touch on something you did or can do well that might help you in this area. So, here, you might write "Mr. Jones is just one teacher, and it feels good to remind myself that I have other teachers I like better."

For the third column, label it "CD" (for cognitive distortion). In this example with Mr. Jones, your distorted thoughts would seem to involve negative filtering and all-or-nothing thinking, so you might write "N. Filt" or "A or N." You could also write "J2C" (for jumping to conclusions), "Cat" (for catastrophizing), "Shoulding" (for "should" thinking), or "NC" (for negative comparison). There may be different cognitive distortions that you experience at the same time. In this activity, just try to spot at least one.

Afterward, reflect on whether coming up with new and helpful thoughts increased your confidence (a healthy, helpful feeling) in your ability to manage and meet these challenges and other ones like them in school. Does challenging your counterproductive self-doubts with more helpful thoughts seem like a good way to break free of them and be ready to do your best?

To recap what you know so far about CBT:

* Just because you have a thought doesn't mean that what the thought is telling you is true.

* Our stress comes partly from the way we interpret events, not just the events themselves (Beck 2018).

* Questioning your unhelpful, inflexible thoughts and replacing them with more reasonable ones can help you feel less stressed out.

* Thinking in more realistic ways about the struggles you face can help you find better ways to cope with them.

Congratulations for having gotten your feet wet with some CBT basics. Your CBT brake lever can decelerate your roller coaster when negative thoughts are running away with you. We'll return to CBT and have you practice using these skills some more in chapter 4. For now, let's introduce you to a second brake lever, positive psychology, which can help you slow down to value yourself more fully and help you find the bright spots in your life.

A Positive Psychology Primer

Positive psychology and CBT both share a central belief that you can use the way you think to help yourself feel better. Positive psychology focuses on three important ways to look at yourself and the world around you:

1. Recognize and value your strengths, talents, and insights.

2. Recognize the situations and events in your life that are going well.

3. Develop and strengthen a positive outlook for the future.

CBT skills are a powerful way to cope with your darker, negative thoughts that lead you to feel stressed out. Positive psychology is a way to further gain hope and work through stress by focusing on the things that are going well in your life. It can slow down your roller coaster by guiding you to recognize your strengths, practice optimism, gain grit, get into a state of "flow," and stay grateful for the good things in your life.

Positive psychology offers some great strategies to help you cope and feel confident when it comes to dealing with stressful situations. Let's start out by considering the role of your strengths.

Strengths

Do you ever take time to think about your talents, your good qualities, and your accomplishments? Focusing on your positive qualities and personal strengths will remind you that you can use them to cope with stressful situations. It'll give you a "can do" attitude, motivating you to push through challenges and overcome them. Wouldn't you like to have the spirit of a champion who gets back up when stress knocks them down?

Try This! Seeing Your Strengths

Look over the following list of strengths that many different teens have identified. Find three that you possess already. If you can think of other strengths you have, what are they?

Enthusiastic	Reliable	Trustworthy
Creative	Disciplined	Patient
Spiritual	Quick learner	Motivated
Determined	Dedicated	Honest
Easygoing	Good communicator	Practical
Flexible	Organized	Detail-oriented
Solid listener	Patient	Open-minded
Humorous	Kind	Caring

I bet it felt good to get in touch with your strengths! Now consider the following questions:

What accomplishments are you most proud of in life, and which strengths helped you achieve them?

Think of the last time you got stressed out. Which one of your strengths might have helped you cope better, if you had reminded yourself to use it?

How can knowing your strengths help you use them in the future?

You can find a separate list of these strengths, The Personal Strengths Summary Sheet, at http://www.newharbinger.com/43911. You may want to print out this list and hang it in a place where you'll see it often, such as on your closet door, clothes dresser, or mirror. You could even make it your home screen on your phone. If you have a car, you could put a short version of it on your dashboard (just don't look at it while you drive!).

Optimism

Optimism is a crucial part of positive psychology. It involves hopefulness and confidence about the future and believing in the chance of a positive outcome during tough times. The power of optimism is evident in a famous quote by Winston Churchill: "A pessimist sees the difficulty in every opportunity; an optimist sees the opportunity in every difficulty." Eternal words of wisdom indeed.

Optimism can help you view stressful times as more manageable. Becoming more optimistic will help you realize that negative events are only temporary, and sooner or later good things happen. It'll help you believe in yourself and your ability to be successful. And it'll help you see that when things don't work out, it's not your fault—it's because circumstances weren't right. This will help you try again!

If you believe that hard work is part of the journey to reach a goal, then failure will seem like nothing more than a hiccup. You'll be more likely to succeed in the future and less stressed out by disappointments. Embracing that persistence, rather than simply relying on your innate talents, is what grit is all about, as you'll start to see next.

Grit

You may think that being good-looking, or being popular or supersmart, is what makes people successful in their lives. Yet according to important research conducted by University of Pennsylvania psychologist Angela Duckworth, a huge predictor of what helps you achieve in life is something called "grit" (Holland 2015). Grit is your ability to persist and bounce back from setbacks as you pursue your goals.

Further, grit empowers you to take reasonable risks (not reckless ones) to face challenges. If you've ever heard the fable about the tortoise and the hare, then you already know about the great things you can achieve by having grit. In that fable, the tortoise and the hare are in a race. The hare sprints ahead but stops midway to take a nap, thereby losing the race. It is the persistence, otherwise known as grit, of the tortoise—even when the initial challenge looked overwhelming—that helped him win the race.

As an example of someone who persisted in the face of challenges, consider the author J. K. Rowling. She personifies grit. Her manuscript for the first Harry Potter book was rejected almost a dozen times.

Have you ever noticed that when you overcome a stressful challenge, you feel stronger? Keeping that in mind can help you persevere, even if there's a chance you may fall short or fail. You can inspire grit in yourself by taking to heart the philosophy that you can achieve successes, both big and small, through dedication and effort. Even if you initially fail to reach a goal, you can continue practicing, training, studying, or doing whatever it is that might eventually get you there. What's really cool is that your brain will grow as you adapt to this new and different path toward your objective.

Flow

Flow is the mental state in which a person performing an activity is totally absorbed in that activity, with a sense of positive and energized focus. When you're in flow, you're so into whatever it is you're doing that you might lose track of time, or the outside world might seem to fall away. Your attention is entirely wrapped up in the moment, and the benefit is that for a while you get a much-needed break from your cares and worries. Some teens find their flow when snowboarding down a mountain, playing a video game, doing a dance routine, drawing a picture, or playing a cool song they really like on a musical instrument.

Gratitude

When you focus on the things in your life that you are grateful for, you'll feel emotionally filled up. By appreciating the good things you have right now, you won't be so focused on what bad things the future might hold. Feeling gratitude can be super-helpful when stress leaves you feeling washed out and empty.

Research shows that gratitude helps people feel calm (Emmons 2010). This may be because when you think about the good stuff that you have in your life and reflect on it with appreciation, the level of your stress hormone, cortisol, which we discussed in the last chapter, decreases.

Here's how some teens describe the benefits of knowing CBT and positive psychology skills.

In Their Own Words

"Learning how to talk myself down when I feel stressed out has helped me handle things *so* much better." **Lisa, age 13**

"I never realized how less stressed out I get when I look at things in a clearer way." **Jerome, age 15**

"My life got so much better when I learned how to focus on the good things and not get so swallowed up in useless, negative thoughts." **Yolanda, age 17**

Remembering your past successes in tough times can really inspire you to cope with current and future stress.

Try This! Seeing the Past Roller Coasters You've Conquered and Survived

Think about something you did that you initially felt nervous about but muddled through somehow. Maybe you were afraid to order food at a restaurant instead of having your parent do it for you. Or maybe you were anxious about those first few days of middle school or high school. What about pushing yourself to go out for a sport at school or to join a club or a community-based organization? Maybe you felt hesitant to join in on social media or video gaming but then you were glad when you did.

What concerns did you have at the time?

After making it through that experience, how did you feel?

Can you think of a few other times you overcame stressful situations?

Do you think you can keep your past personal triumphs in mind as you face whatever makes you nervous nowadays?

Putting It All Together

In this chapter, you learned that you can survive and cope with stress by getting some tools from CBT and positive psychology under your belt. CBT skills can help you manage your reacting brain, and positive psychology gives you strategies that make use of your thinking brain to help you feel more fulfilled. Noticing and reevaluating your stressed-out thoughts, and keeping your strengths and what you're capable of in mind as you move through life, can help you transform a situation that's stressful—one where you think *This sucks!*—and turn it into something that's tolerable or even positive. While many teens I've known prefer to turn to CBT skills first and positive psychology second, your personal preference counts most for what will work best for you. So please know it's okay to reach for whichever brake lever feels most helpful in the moment.

In the next chapter, you'll learn more about CBT and how to practice using it.

PART 2

Using CBT Skills to Slow Down the Roller Coaster

chapter 4

Noticing, Evaluating, and Changing Your Distorted Negative Thoughts

The greatest weapon against stress is our ability to choose one thought over another.

—William James

Demanding and seemingly impossible situations rev up our reacting brains with upsetting thoughts. These negative, exaggerated, and rigid ways of thinking are often, unfortunately, automatic. They can jolt you into feeling stressed out and make you fear the worst. If you look back on times when you felt really anxious, sad, frustrated, or angry (as in the chapter 1 activity), you might recognize that your thoughts were over the top, making the situation seem worse than it turned out to be. You may have convinced yourself that your life was over, but seeing as how you're reading this now, that clearly wasn't the case!

A big part of how CBT works is that once you examine your negative thoughts (also known as negative self-talk) and swap them out for friendlier, more helpful ones, you'll start to feel better. Sadly, during times of stress, we often don't pay enough attention to our negative thoughts to realize how much they rattle us. They can be like "invisible" stealth bombers, so we don't know we're under attack until we're dealing with the physical explosions and emotional fallout they create. Or, to stick with the roller-coaster metaphor, we don't realize we're steadily accelerating until we're about to break the sound barrier.

In the previous chapter, you learned how your body signals you when you're feeling overwhelmed. Now that you know that your body reacts by tensing up in response to stress, these signals can be your cue to scan the skies within your mind and look for the thoughts that are trying to fly under your radar. Once you spot them, you can intercept them. Or, in keeping with the roller-coaster idea, you can calculate a more reasonable velocity and pull the brake lever to calm your body and settle your mind.

All it takes is a little practice, and you'll see that your new CBT brake lever is powerful and easy to apply. Once you get better at noticing your negative thoughts, you can change them to helpful ones, giving you a trusty, reliable way to regain control in times of stress. You do this by using your prefrontal cortex (your thinking brain) to evaluate, challenge, and change those thoughts.

Upsetting Thoughts Get in Our Way

To recap the connection between negative thoughts, negative feelings, and counterproductive behaviors, check out Tasha's story. Tasha was struggling with social anxiety that totally stressed her out. See if you can recognize the types of negative thoughts (and feelings) she had.

Tasha's Story

Tasha had intense physical reactions to the idea of going to a party, especially when her friend kept bringing it up at her house one day. Her face got hot, there were butterflies in her stomach, and she started to feel dizzy. These sensations seemed to come out of the blue, until she remembered that they were her typical signals of stress. So she excused herself from the room and started to tune in to her thoughts. They went like this: My friend wants me to go with her to this really cool party, but what if everyone notices how awkward I am? Ugh, there's no way I can do this! I'll definitely say something stupid, and people will just think I'm a lame weirdo loser. Everyone can enjoy parties so easily and laugh with their friends, but I stand in the corner like a nervous wreck. I'd rather sit at home than be humiliated. *These negative thoughts were based on the rigid belief that she was a loser who was incapable of making successful connections at a party. The feelings they led to were anxiety and a strong sense of guilt.*

Would you say that Tasha was catastrophizing, jumping to conclusions, and making negative comparisons? As you can see from Tasha's example, it's super-important to learn to recognize alarming negative thoughts so that they don't lead to stress and get in the way of your plans and responsibilities. Tasha's bodily reactions show how when stressful situations and events occur, your reacting brain jumps into fight, flight, or freeze mode (resulting in inaccurate, negative thoughts), producing upsetting feelings and behaviors that may not serve you well—in Tasha's case, she decided not to go to the party and missed out on a good time. Later in this chapter, you'll see how to evaluate and challenge distorted negative thought patterns with clearer ways of thinking.

Let's now take a look at common stressful situations for teens that trigger negative thoughts and feelings. Next, we'll discuss how to tune in and consciously notice your upsetting thoughts in these types of situations. Then, we'll have you practice using your thinking brain to evaluate, challenge, and change your thoughts and feelings.

Common Triggers

The common stress triggers that tend to rile up teens' reacting brains and lead them to upsetting thoughts fall into four main categories: academic, social, body image, and family.

Academic Triggers

* Taking a difficult class

* Hearing peers make comments comparing their academic performance with your own

* Being presented new class material that you can't grasp even when it's further explained

* Failing to do homework/readings and falling behind

* Cramming for an exam

* Receiving a poor grade on a test or project

* Having your teacher criticize or correct your work

Social Triggers

* Not knowing what "group" you belong in

* Trying to fit into a group

* Judging yourself based on your peers' opinions

* Feeling as though peers are superior to you

* Lack of attention from people you're romantically interested in

* Rejection from people you're romantically interested in

* Fighting with or being ignored by a friend(s)

* Being ignored or not being invited to an event on social
media

* Relationship issues/turbulence (breakups/fights)

Body-Image Triggers

* Comparing yourself with peers who have "better" bodies

* Comparing the way you look in trendy clothes with the
way your peers look "better" in the same kind of clothes

* Focusing on a facial or bodily feature that you dislike

* Changing up your look (haircut/wardrobe) but feeling
even more self-conscious

* Focusing on your physical appearance more than on your
well-being

* Pressure from peers to diet or work out rigorously

Family Triggers

* Your parent asking you about something you haven't done
yet (homework, finishing a project, applying for college,
etc.)

* Your sibling belittling, rejecting, or excluding you

* Comparing yourself with your siblings in terms of accomplishments, appearances, and so on

* Your parents fighting and/or stress over divorce

* Chronic illness and/or death of a loved one

* Addiction

* Financial issues

Now that you've reviewed the types of stress triggers that many teens face, give the following activity a try to learn more about what types of triggers send your own reacting brain speeding down the track.

Try This! Identifying Your Stress Triggers

Quiet your mind by taking a few deep breaths. Now reflect on the list of stress triggers above (or download and print the Common Stress Triggers Summary Sheet at http://www.newharbinger.com/43911) as you consider the following questions:

* Which of the above triggers did you recognize as ones that stress you out personally?

* Do your stress triggers tend to occur in one area (academic, social, body image, or family) more than the rest?

* Can you think of any other areas of your life that stress you out? What are some triggers for you in these areas?

* What types of physical reactions accompany these stressful situations?

Taking the time to identify and reflect on your stress triggers, as you just did, is a huge step in learning how to manage stressful situations in your life. The more conscious you are of what events tend to upset you, the easier it'll be to evaluate and challenge your negative thoughts whenever these events occur. This is how you pull your CBT brake lever when your roller coaster is moving too fast for comfort.

Tuning In to Negative Thoughts

When all kinds of stressors are coming at you, your reacting brain puts you in fight, flight, or freeze mode. This is what creates those distorted thoughts that spawn intense emotions. You're probably used to focusing only on your emotions when you feel stressed out (and maybe blaming yourself or others for "making" you feel that way). When you actively engage your prefrontal cortex (your thinking brain), however, you can evaluate and challenge the real culprits—those negative thoughts that really hyped up your emotions. Then, you can replace them with calming ones. But first, you should refamiliarize yourself with the most common types of negative thoughts (to help you spot such distorted thoughts for what they are).

Let's now take a detailed look at the negative thought patterns we first mentioned in chapter 3. As you read about each of these distorted ways of thinking, reflect on the ways in which you may struggle with it. Rest assured that when it comes to the way we think in stressful situations, we can all be our worst adversary.

Common Types of Negative Thoughts

CBT, as you probably now understand, involves learning to identify and challenge your negative thoughts. Being able to catch your brain in the act of creating unhelpful, unreasonable ways of thinking is key to being able to deal with them. Following are the types of negative thoughts that teens most often experience. Any of them can really stress you out, as well as lead you to treat yourself (and others!) unfairly.

*   *All-or-nothing thinking.* If you often use the word "always," "never," or "constantly," you might tend to have a polarized way of seeing things. For example, your friend *never* thinks about anyone but herself, your teacher is *totally* unfair, your sibling is *always* favored over you, or you *never* know how to make a good impression. Such statements are too extreme to be true. This inflexible way of thinking can influence you to see yourself, others, and situations in highly negative ways, because it makes the situation seem hopeless. For example, you need to remember that you *did* make a good impression at some point in the past, even if it was only once, so you can do it again!

*   *Jumping to conclusions.* Are you often certain that a situation is going to turn out poorly, before things even have a chance to play out? If you hear your teacher announce a test and immediately think, *I'm gonna fail this test*, then you're jumping to conclusions. The same goes for telling yourself you won't be able to stand your mother's new boyfriend, even though you haven't met him yet.

*   *Negative filtering.* When you look only at the negatives of a situation even though there are positives to be seen, then you're falling victim to negative filtering. Exaggerating, magnifying, or obsessing about the things that didn't go well leads to sadness, anxiety, and stress. An example of negative filtering is, when remembering a past relationship, thinking only about the bad times and the mistakes

you made instead of also considering the good times and how the relationship helped you grow.

* *Catastrophizing.* This type of thought pattern occurs when you take a potentially minor issue and make it into a majorly disastrous one. Asking "What if...?" often sets the stage for this distorted way of thinking. For example, a teen who gets a rejection from one college she applied to may immediately think no other colleges will accept her and thus her life is ruined. She may say to herself, *What if don't get into any college, I become homeless, and my friends and family think I'm a loser?* As another example, if you make a joke and it doesn't go over well, you may panic that no one will ever find you cool to hang out with.

* *"Should" (or "should not") thinking.* Most people don't like being pressured, and I assume you feel this way too. "Should" thinking involves very strict expectations about how you and others must behave. For example, you may think a friend *should* do a favor for you because you did one for him. But "keeping score" in relationships in this way can really create resentment. As another example, you may think you *should not* have any body-image concerns (because the people you look up to don't seem to) and that if you do, then something must be wrong with your body. In this case, you'd be giving yourself a highly unreason- able standard that will likely make you feel alone and shamed. When it comes to your responsibilities, there's a difference between (a) being conscientious, or motivat- ing yourself, and (b) making yourself feel like crap. For example, the thought *I should study harder* is likely to lead

you to feel burned out or worn down, and you'll end up *less* motivated.

* *Labeling.* Sadly, we tend to unfairly label many people— both ourselves and others. Seeing yourself as "stupid" because you can't readily grasp a new concept in your math class is an example of this. So is seeing the new kid as a "loser" just because he wears fashions from the last decade.

* *Negative comparisons.* Walking down school hallways and seeing attractive peers, hearing about others who received higher grades, or having a sibling who seems to have an easy life may lead you to feel lousy if you compare your situation with theirs. Knowing your value because of who you are and who you want to be will lead you to less stress compared with trying to be like your seemingly perfect peers. After all, even your peers who seem to have it made are struggling with the same sort of pressures you are facing in many areas of life (more on this in chapter 9).

Now that you've taken a closer look at counterproductive thinking patterns, let's discuss learning how to notice them throughout the day.

Negative Thoughts Lead to Upset Feelings

As you continue to become aware of your negative thought patterns by reflecting on them, you'll see that there are many types of upsetting feelings that come along for the ride on your roller coaster of stress. Check out the list of feelings that are often linked to the negative thinking patterns described above:

Angry	Defeated	Sad	Hurt
Insecure	Detached	Anxious	Stuck
Ashamed	Embarrassed	Humiliated	Hateful
Frustrated	Hopeless	Discouraged	Rejected
Disgusted	Annoyed	Overwhelmed	Lazy
Judged	Aggressive	Self-defeating	Scared
Suspicious	Jealous	Impatient	Impulsive

The following activity will help you practice tuning in to your negative thoughts and related upset feelings.

Try This! Noticing Your Negative Thoughts and Feelings

Take a few relaxing breaths and clear your mind. Now think about something that upset you recently (e.g., over the past few weeks) and ask yourself the following questions:

What was the situation that triggered your stress?

What signals was your body sending you?

What negative thoughts came into your mind? Do they fit one of the types we've discussed? (You can look back at the list or refer to the Distorted Negative Thoughts Summary Sheet at http://www.newhar binger.com/43911.)

How did your negative thoughts lead you to feel?

Did those feelings lead you to do something that, in hindsight, may have been counterproductive?

You can use the worksheet entitled Tracking Bodily Symptoms and Counterproductive Thoughts and Feelings to help you practice tracking your bodily symptoms discussed in the last chapter as they relate to your negative thoughts and feelings over time. It can be accessed at http://www.newharbinger .com/43911. You can keep this worksheet taped to a wall in your room (or folded inside your journal, if you keep one) and check in with yourself a few times a week, or even more often at first, to see how and where stress is impacting you. (As you get better at putting on the brakes, you may no longer need to track your thoughts and bodily symptoms as closely or as frequently.) Try not to think of this as "work." Think of it as practice for lowering your stress, which will save you time and energy both in the coming days and in the long run.

As you become more able to notice your negative thoughts, the next step in CBT is to evaluate and challenge them. Once you can do this, they won't influence your feelings and behaviors as much.

The way to evaluate your upsetting, irrational, rigid, or unhelpful thoughts is to look for any evidence that supports them. In order to deserve being treated as true, a thought needs more than just a feeling that it probably *is* true. It also isn't enough that a thought simply fits with certain beliefs you have about the world. To begin to challenge your own negative thoughts, try the following activity.

Try This! Evaluating Your Negative Thoughts

Take a few minutes and reflect on something in your life that's stressing you out (maybe in the academic, social, body-image, or family arena). Now look over the list of negative thought patterns in this chapter (or see the Distorted Negative Thoughts Summary Sheet, at http://www.newharbinger.com/43911). Pick a pattern that seems tied to why you're feeling stressed, anxious, or unhappy about this situation. (You may find this exercise more helpful if you write out a particular negative thought that you have and then answer the questions below on a separate piece of paper or in a journal.) Consider the following:

Which negative thought pattern is associated with this situation?

What, as near as you can tell, is the exact wording of your negative thought?

What bodily reactions and emotions (e.g., sadness, anger, frustration, anxiety) occur for you as a result of thinking in this way?

Can you see how this way of thinking feeds negative feelings that increase your stress?

What solid evidence is there to support this way of thinking? For example, if you have the thought *I will fail this test*, how can you know that for sure—have you taken the exact same test, failed it, and learned nothing new since then (highly unlikely, I imagine)?

Might another person in your life look at this situation differently or with a different belief?

What's the worst-case scenario based on the facts you know about this situation, and how likely is that to happen?

Go back to the negative thought you originally came up with or wrote down. Does it seem less true than it did at the start of this activity? Evaluating your negative thoughts can feel really empowering, right? It diminishes their intensity and force.

John, a high-school junior, described the value of learning to tune in to his negative thoughts and evaluate them.

John's Story

People kept saying to me that junior year is so important for getting into college. It seemed ridiculous how often people went off about it. Like, duh, okay, yeah, I get it—junior year is a big deal.

What was crazy, though, was how I let the pressure get to me. I was like, "Yeah, what if I don't do well enough in my classes?" "What if I blow it this year?" I was moody and became super-worried about getting into college. And I took so much of my stress out on my mom. I was being really difficult with her, and when she would try to help I just was rude because I felt so overwhelmed. I kinda feel bad about it now.

Actually, I was blaming everyone else for creating that pressure and stress, but then I learned about CBT and how messed-up some of my thoughts got. Even though I couldn't stop people around me from saying things, I realized that how I thought about it all was making things much worse. Like, I had this crazy thought that I was a total failure just because I was having a hard time with honors chemistry. With CBT, I was able to see how tense and crazed I felt when thinking that and how ridiculous it was. Now I just tell myself that not all things are going to come easily to me and that this is not the end of the world.

With your CBT brake lever at hand, you can learn to change your self-talk, just like John did, to help you manage your stress too.

Rethinking Your Negative Thoughts

Now that you've had some practice identifying and evaluating your upsetting thoughts, the next step is to change them to helpful, productive ones that engender better feelings. By flexing your thinking brain *now*—when, hopefully, you're not too stressed—you can learn to come up with healthy, alternative self-talk to challenge your negative beliefs in difficult situations as they come your way.

To get you ready, here are some of examples of negative thoughts and the feelings that go with them. The type(s) that best fit(s) each thought appears in parentheses, because knowing what kind of thought you're having can really help you come up with one that'll defuse this potential bomb. Below that, related to the same situation, is an example of a helpful response and the positive feeling it would probably foster.

* *She just dumped me, and I'll never find another girlfriend. I feel hopeless.* (All-or-nothing thinking)

   "I'm disappointed and feel pretty upset right now. Yet maturely handling this rejection helps me feel confident that I'll meet someone else who values me."

* *This quiz is ridiculously hard. There's no way I can pass this class, and I feel like a total failure.* (Jumping to conclusions)

   "Okay, yes, this one was tough. Now I know, however, to prepare more and have a better sense of what this teacher expects. This helps me feel relieved and encouraged."

* *I can't believe I made these dumb mistakes on this math test that got in the way of crushing it. I'm so disappointed!* (Negative filtering)

   "I got an 83 on this test, even with some mistakes. It's pretty cool that I understand the key concepts. I actually feel kinda happy about it."

* *What if I can't get this project done in time and it ruins my grade in the class? I'm so worried.* (Catastrophizing)

   "The worst thing that can happen is that I'll have to work this out with my teacher. Starting to lay out what I have to do to get this done will be much more helpful right now than worrying. I actually feel psyched now."

* *I should be able to ignore those hurtful things being said about me on social media, but I just can't put it out of my head. I feel weak for not being able to handle this.* ("Should" thinking and labeling)

"Expecting to not feel anything isn't fair to myself. I'm going to cut myself some slack for getting upset and reach out to some friends for support. I'm feeling stronger knowing I'm dealing with it."

* *I'm such a fat, lazy loser, and I can't make any friends. I feel so ashamed and alone.* (Labeling)

"Beating myself up over my weight only makes me feel worse. My personality counts a lot more than my weight for making and keeping friends. I feel pride in not being as obsessed as other people seem to be with looking perfect."

* *My sister doesn't seem to have to study at all and gets an A, whereas I have to bust my butt to get a B. I hate to admit it, but I'm totally jealous of her.* (Negative comparison)

"People tell me I have a good work ethic, and that'll serve me well now and down the road. Actually, I feel kinda proud of myself for acknowledging that I feel threatened by my sister and for working on it."

Now that you've reviewed the examples, it's time to put on your thinking cap. As you approach the next activity, it may be helpful to think of it as learning to debate your distorted negative thoughts with helpful thoughts that have a better basis in reality. The good news is that you'll always win these debates, because negative thoughts are irrational and fueled by worry. Helpful thoughts are rational and based on logic and evidence.

Here are some tips to help you effectively dispute your negative thoughts.

* To challenge the thought that something "always" or "never" happens (all-or-nothing thinking), describe what "tends to" happen.

* As a healthier alternative to a "What if?" question (catastrophizing), come up with an answer to "What's the worst that can honestly happen?" or start your response by adding "so" to the question: "So what if...?"

* Instead of describing yourself or others as "lazy," "stupid," or "selfish" (labeling), you can say "less motivated," "not yet prepared," or "self-concerned."

As we've discussed, practicing your CBT skills will help you make your brake stronger. Here's a practice opportunity for you.

Try This! Challenging Your Distorted Thoughts

On a separate piece of paper or in a journal (or using the worksheet available at http://www.newharbinger.com/43911), create three columns. You can label them as shown below. Think of some of the negative things you say to yourself in times of stress, and list them in the first column. Try to identify how each one makes you feel. In the second column, for each negative thought, write out a more rational thought that wins the debate. If you're having difficulty coming up with a response, look back at the examples or come back to it later. In the third column, write the feeling(s) your new way of thinking might lead you to have in each case.

Negative Thought/ Feeling	Helpful Alternative Thought	Resulting Healthier Feeling(s)

Was it easy or difficult to come up with helpful thoughts?

Did this activity feel like a chore, or did it feel empowering?

Did taking the time to write out your negative thoughts, evaluate them, and challenge them help you feel more in control of your thoughts and emotions?

Does coming up with more reasonable ways to think about the situation seem like something you can do when you feel stressed out?

The more you practice identifying, challenging, and changing your negative thoughts, the easier it'll be for you to do whenever stressors arise. At times, however, you may feel so emotionally flooded that it feels impossible to find and reach for your brake lever.

What If I'm Too Stressed Out to Use CBT Skills?

When the walls are closing in and you feel overpowered by stress, it may not seem possible for you to notice, evaluate, and change your thoughts. On the contrary! It's the perfect time to use CBT skills—just start by focusing on your breathing to help you calm down.

Deep breathing can be a really helpful way to settle your mind. It's a fundamental exercise in mindfulness. *Mindfulness* involves gaining awareness of what's going on in your mind and body in the here and now. Focusing on the present is one way to help yourself stop worrying about the future or brooding over the past. And taking a minute to get in touch with your body is great for helping you get a little freedom from the thoughts on your mind. Because you're always breathing, you can always just think about your breathing *more*, in order to think about other stuff *less*. As a bonus, the sensations of breathing tend to be mildly pleasant—or, at least, not uncomfortable!

Try This! Being Mindful by Noticing Your Breath

To prepare for this activity, simply find a quiet place and sit comfortably. Once you're settled, if it feels right to you, let your eyes gently close. Or you can gaze softly at a spot a few feet in front of you, looking at nothing in particular.

1. Focus your attention on your breath.

2. Place one hand on your chest and one on your belly to help you notice taking a full breath.

3. Gently breathe in deeply, saying to yourself, *I'm breathing in.*

4. Pay attention to the sensations of your breath passing into your body.

5. As you breathe out, say to yourself, *I'm breathing out.*

6. Observe the sensations in your body related to your out-breath.

7. Notice whether your attention is still on your breath or whether it has wandered to thoughts about other things.

8. If your attention has wandered, gently return your awareness to your breath.

9. Repeat steps 3 through 8 four times.

Now, reflect on what was it like to pay attention to your breath and the sensations of it passing through your body. What was it like for you to come back to the present moment when you noticed your attention had wandered? Did you become aware of anything interesting or surprising? Can you see how this activity offers you a soothing way to take a "breather" from upsetting thoughts and be in a better position to evaluate them?

I recommend doing some mindful breathing not only when you feel overwhelmed, but also at other times, when you're chill. You may want to take a few mindful breaths in the morning before going to school, to help set the tone for a more relaxed day. As stressors and upsetting thoughts pop up throughout the day, you can take some mindful breaths to re-center yourself and then evaluate your thoughts.

But Can't Negative Thinking Help Me?

Have you known kids who say things like "I'm totally going to fail this test" but end up doing great? If you have, then you may think that underestimating your abilities or making yourself stressed out with harshly negative thoughts can be a good way to motivate yourself. You may even believe that having an irrational fear of getting dumped, bombing on a test, not making the team, or doing badly in a recital will help you keep your options open, study hard, hone your skills, or practice your routine. At the very least, you'll be protected from disappointment (to a certain extent) if your negative prediction comes true, because you were right all along. And who wants to be around someone with obnoxious swag (aka excessive self-esteem)? So it can't hurt, right?

But it can. Getting yourself all worked up and bent out of shape will take a toll on you (and those around you), as discussed in chapter 2. Indulging in irrational, negative thoughts can make you super-anxious, sad, angry, and unreasonably discouraged.

Deliberately thinking negatively can also lead you away from better ways to cope with situations that you struggle with. As you'll discover in the next chapter, combining healthy thoughts and feelings with healthy coping behaviors will give you the best balance of managing stress and facing the challenges that come your way.

Putting It All Together

You've already covered a lot of ground. In this chapter, you learned to notice your stress triggers. You uncovered their link to your distorted negative thoughts, and you learned how to evaluate and challenge those thoughts with healthier ways to look at stressful situations. The more you practice listening to your body and noticing your thoughts, the easier it'll be to slow down your roller coaster of stress with CBT skills.

Next, we'll discuss how knowing and drawing on a range of problem-solving behaviors is another part of using your CBT skills. Managing your thoughts and feelings with the tools presented in this chapter will help you find better ways of coping with stress than either lashing out or bottling it up.

chapter 5

Choosing Helpful Coping Behaviors

You've learned that as you face difficult challenges and obstacles, stress comes your way when your reacting brain creates irrational, counter-productive thoughts. This happens because your fight, flight, or freeze response kicks in. You now have the powerful CBT skills to spot, evaluate, and change those over-the-top upsetting thoughts and to feel better as a result. But, no matter how much you change your thoughts to be more reasonable and helpful, you still need to purposely behave in ways that guide you to remain calm and take action to overcome stressful problems.

Calming behaviors and problem-solving strategies are the focus of this chapter. Both can be super-helpful for getting through demanding and difficult situations. Calming behaviors will help you maintain your helpful thoughts and feel positive emotions when you face stressful situations. Problem-solving strategies (we'll use the terms "behaviors," "actions," and "strategies" interchangeably) will get you moving to figure out how to manage demanding tasks and situations. Using the coping behaviors described in this chapter is a big part of applying your CBT brake lever on the roller coaster of stress.

Check out the diagram that follows. It shows the significant role that helpful coping behaviors play in managing stress.

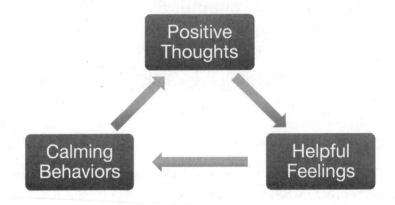

The Cycle of Positive Thoughts, Feelings, and Behaviors

Do you notice the similarity to the cycle of negative thoughts, feelings, and actions in chapter 3? As you can see, calming behaviors play an essential role in the cycle of managing stress. Once you think in more effective ways and have more helpful feelings, applying positive coping strategies (to keep you calm) will spur even more positive thoughts and feelings.

The importance of taking effective actions when facing stressful times is huge for you as a teen. To help raise your awareness of how much your coping behaviors count in stressful times, try the following activity.

Try This! Valuing Your Calming Behaviors

Think about a stressful time you faced within the last few months when you felt caught off guard and not sure how to handle the situation. This could pertain to schoolwork, experiences with friends or other peers, or circumstances within your family. Then reflect on these questions:

Did you overly focus on your thoughts and feelings at the time?

Did you take any steps to keep yourself calm? If so, what did you do, and how much did it help?

If you truly didn't know what to do to help yourself feel less stressed, what are some ideas for next time?

Proactively reflecting on coping behaviors to use in stressful times will keep them more accessible in your mind to calm you when you need them. As you read this chapter, why not take note of the coping behaviors that seem good to you?

What follows are ways to keep your roller coaster from speeding out of control by helping you calm down and solve problems. We'll first discuss several calming behaviors. Next, we'll discuss problem-solving strategies, which are designed to help you tackle the challenges and obstacles that come your way. There are certainly many additional coping strategies for managing stress. The ones presented here, however, tend to be very helpful for teens.

You may already do some of these positive coping behaviors. If so, great! Others will likely be totally new to you. Maybe you can decide on one strategy that works well for you and will be your "go to" but you'll consider giving others a try as well. Perhaps certain strategies will work better in certain situations.

Most teens find these strategies to be quick and easy to use and highly comforting when they're stressed out. These calming and problem-solving behaviors can also prevent you from feeling stressed out in the first place.

Please check out these super-important stress-management strategies with an open mind. The more you use them, the better they'll work, because training your brain to really learn these new tricks requires repetition. And some of them may seem corny, but why limit yourself when it comes to ways to combat stress?

Calming Behaviors

When you're all wound up, using a calming behavior can stop you from saying something mean and regretting it. It can keep you from feeling like you need to go into (or stay in) silent-treatment mode. It can prevent you from injuring your hand and getting in trouble by punching a wall. It's also a much more cost-saving and practical choice than hurling your mobile device on the ground! So take the time to teach yourself ten teen-tested strategies for putting those urges to rest.

1. Breathe with a Calming Image

In chapter 4, we talked about mindful breathing as a way of collecting yourself to challenge your upsetting thoughts. You can use mindful breathing as described in that activity in almost any situation when stress is getting the better of you.

A variation of mindful breathing is to pair it with a calming image, which you can try in the upcoming activity. For example, if you love going to the beach, you can mindfully breathe in and out while visualizing the waves rolling in. Maybe you find mountains enchanting to gaze at and you wish to imagine some snow-capped peaks. Or, if you like going on hikes in the woods, then visualizing a relaxing trail that winds through some gently rustling trees may feel very calming. Perhaps you would rather visualize a clear blue sky or clouds passing by. Whatever image you use, pairing it with some mindful breathing can be a real stress-buster. In the following activity, you'll imagine a magnificent tree. Give it a try and see how it feels.

Try This! Branching Out from Your Breath

Close your eyes and picture a strong, large tree, filled with bright green leaves. Breathe in gently through your nose, mindfully feeling your breath moving down to your abdomen. As you do so, visualize yourself connected to the ground like the roots of the tree. Now breathe out gently through your mouth, observing the sensations of your breath traveling the opposite direction. As you do so, picture yourself letting go of your stressful thoughts and feelings. Repeat two times.

Now envision some strong winds coming toward and blowing on the tree. Imagine these winds represent the stressors (e.g., concerns over how you look or act, school struggles, social pressures, extracurricular burdens, or family issues) that come your way. Notice how the tree bends with the wind but doesn't break. It's still standing tall, and it isn't going anywhere. Infuse yourself with the stability and strength of this tree as you continue to breathe. Gently try to hold that image (the tree's strength and how it's also present in you) in your mind for about thirty seconds to a minute, or six to twelve breath cycles. As you think of this strong yet flexible tree, accept whatever thoughts, sensations, or emotions blow your way.

Afterward, think about how it felt to identify with the strength and flexibility of the tree:

> Did visualizing the tree lower your stress more than mindful breathing alone?
>
> Did focusing on the tree soothe you by giving you a sense of strength and confidence?
>
> Did noticing the size and strength of the tree make the intensity of your stress feel weaker and more manageable?
>
> What other visualizations of nature might lower the intensity of your stress?

As a way to vary and expand this activity, imagine the sun setting over the mountains, the beach, or another distant horizon while you breathe in and out, and watch your stress go down as the sun fades. Or, try breathing while imagining and taking in the vastness of a starry night.

2. Count to Ten

You've probably heard it said that counting to ten is an effective way to cool your anger or other emotions. Counting to ten gives you two things that you likely don't feel you have when you're overwhelmed by stress: (a) more time and (b) a helpful distraction from whatever's upsetting you. Focusing on the numbers switches your neural activity from your reacting brain to your thinking brain. This takes your mind off what's triggering you and gives you a chance to better deal with difficulties you're facing. So the next time you're feeling stressed out, try counting silently. In the event you're talking with someone (or texting, or chatting online) while needing to count to ten, politely excuse yourself. (We'll talk more about managing conflict in chapter 9.)

3. Take a "Feel Good" Break

When you engage in an activity that feels enjoyable, you have fewer negative thoughts. And when it comes to calming yourself down, fewer thoughts are the way to go. There are many brief and pleasurable activities that can give you an enjoyable and calming break from stress. Following are some suggestions. You can do these activities for anywhere from a minute or two to an hour or so, depending on the level of stress you're experiencing and the time you have available.

* Doodle a cool design.

* Think something positive about yourself.

* Adjust to a straighter posture.

* Draw a picture.

* Make a quick list of your past accomplishments.

* Mentally smile at someone and send it their way.

* Give your pet some attention.

* Listen to music.

* Play a video game (just don't let this one become too frequent and overly consuming).

4. Reach Out When You Feel Stressed Out

There's a famous quote by English writer John Donne (1572–1631): "No man is an island." One way of interpreting this is that we don't feel good or fare very well when we feel alone and isolated. This is especially true when we feel stressed out. Seeking emotional support from others can be very helpful in reducing stress, because it can make you feel as though you've got someone in your corner. It can also give you some distance from, or a different perspective on, your problems.

Being alone in your stress can leave you bottled up with it. But venting to others can help you avoid emotionally exploding or imploding. So when you feel stressed out, try texting or talking to a friend, a family member, or someone else you trust. If no one's available, you may want to write your thoughts and feelings down on a sheet of paper or in a journaling app. Giving a pet some affection can provide a sense of companionship and safe, nonjudgmental support, too.

There may be times when the stressful things you're going through warrant getting professional support. These include feeling anxiety or depression symptoms, feeling suicidal, being in an abusive relationship, struggling with an addiction, or being a family member of someone who's battling an addiction or some kind of mental illness. If any of this is going on or ever becomes the case for you, please speak to your parents or another caring, reliable adult and arrange to see a qualified mental health professional.

5. Get Your Body Moving

Doing some exercise will increase the flow and/or effect of your brain's feel-good neurotransmitters, called endorphins. These are what give athletes their "natural high." Exercise is also really cool because moving and focusing on your body gets you tuned in to the present moment, which helps you break away from worries about the past or the future. Walking or running casually or for time or distance, lifting weights, or doing any other kind of physical activity gives you a sense of accomplishment too. The bottom line is that the more you move, the less stressed you'll probably feel.

6. Use a Calming, Affirming Mantra

A mantra is a slogan or phrase you repeat to yourself, silently or out loud. Mantras can be very soothing and centering because they help quiet all the other thoughts buzzing around in your head. Below are examples of affirmations (self-supporting statements) to repeat to yourself, which you can try out and use if they feel helpful:

* "I have strength and dignity."

* "I'm learning and growing from my setbacks."

* "I know my value."

* "Stepping back helps me step forward."

* "This is not the end of the world."

The word "mantra" comes to us from the ancient language of Sanskrit, from a word meaning "sacred counsel." With that in mind, what sacred counsel or timeless wisdom would you like to hear in times of stress? If you could go to the proverbial mountaintop, what message of positive acceptance would you hope to receive there? Check out the next activity to deliver it to your own ears.

Try This! Practicing a Mantra

Reflect on your upsetting thoughts and feelings from a recent difficult situation. Or think of something a friend or peer had to deal with that was stressful to them and that could be stressful to you as well. Reflect on how you're feeling as you imagine yourself in this situation. Now select a mantra from the above list, or use one of your own.

Repeat your chosen phrase calmly and slowly three times (if you have some privacy, say the words out loud) as you continue to consider the difficulties involved with the situation that came to mind.

Did saying the mantra feel calming?

Did it give you a sense of empowerment, or maybe a feeling that you could start to address the problem?

Could using a mantra at the time have helped prevent you from getting stressed out?

Using a mantra on a regular basis may help you feel emotionally stronger and even more physically relaxed. Try it whenever you're about to do something challenging, like starting your homework after school. There may be times you'll prefer to say it out loud for extra effect, but you can always say it gently to yourself. Just do what feels best at the time.

7. Crack Yourself Up

Laughing gives you a release from stress by quickly changing your perspective from being in a crisis to feeling a fresh new attitude. In addition, it reduces cortisol, your stress hormone, and strengthens your immune system, which helps promote overall good health (Mayo Clinic Staff n.d.; Scott 2018b).

Here are some ways to get laughing:

* Watch an online clip of babies laughing.

* Watch videos of pets doing amusing tricks.

* Reflect on fun times with family or friends.

* Try to force yourself to keep a straight face while saying, "ha ha ha, ho, ho, ho, hee, hee, hee!" out loud.

* Run around the house pretending that you're driving your "happy bus." (This one may be better if you're home alone, so that your family members don't think you're "losing it"!)

8. Draw a Mandala

Mandalas are any type of circular design drawn from the middle and progressively moving outward. Throughout history and across religions, mandalas have been seen as very soothing and calming. You can start by drawing a very small circle on the center of a blank piece of paper and drawing larger and larger concentric circles to fill up the page. Or you can make any kind of circular design (e.g., slightly wavy circles or circles with distinct little zigzags). As another design tweak, incorporating your own interests can infuse this exercise with added personal meaning. Some teens like to draw things representing their interests and use a series of them to create the circles for the mandala (flowers, tennis rackets, baseballs, etc.).

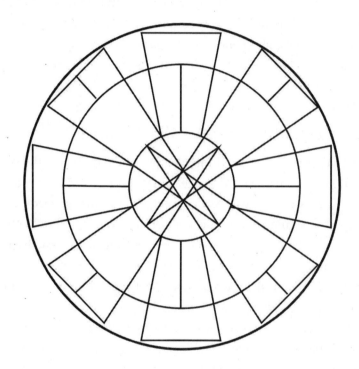

9. Get Enough Sleep and Rest

I know, you probably have heard this at least a hundred times before. But ask yourself honestly how often you feel tired or down-right exhausted. Feeling tired can lower your ability to manage stress, because it makes it harder for you to think straight. Your thinking brain needs a surprising amount of energy. Getting enough sleep and rest increases your energy level, improves your memory, increases your ability to absorb new information, and helps your body restore itself. Going to bed at a reasonable hour may be important in this regard, as well as avoiding bright lights from screens and other sources close to bedtime, (put your mobile device out of reach, so that you're not tempted to reach for it) because light tricks your brain into thinking it needs to stay awake.

10. Remember, "You Are What You Eat"

It's said that what you think, you become (and this is the core of CBT). If you haven't heard that one, you've probably heard the similar saying "You are what you eat." It really is true that a steady diet of junk food is similar to a steady diet of negative thoughts. Both will catch up with you and leave you feeling depleted of physical drive and creative energy. Eating or drinking something with a lot of sugar or caffeine may seem like a good way to get moving to do a boring or even complex task, but it can end up leading to a rebound feeling of low energy. In contrast, eating healthy, nourishing meals, or having a warm cup of herbal tea or bowl of good soup when you're feeling stressed, will set the stage to calm you down. This is a far better option than a sugary or caffeine-loaded beverage that'll likely leave you wound up and maybe even agitated. If you've just gotta have that hot chocolate or ice cream once in a while, that's okay, but how about just one packet or scoop instead of two?

Hopefully, soon you can reflect on how you found relief from stress by using effective coping behaviors, like these two teens.

In Their Own Words

"Sometimes I get so many emotions going on in my head that I want to cry, but when I take a few deep breaths and picture something calming, it helps me stop thinking about these things so much." **James, age 14**

"It's annoying when my parents remind me that how smooth my life feels is based on the choices I make when I'm stressed out—but, yeah, I'm not gonna lie—after I count to ten, I realize they're pretty much right! Sometimes I even laugh at myself, which lightens me up to then see how stubborn I can be." **Timothy, age 16**

Now that we've looked at how to calm down and promote a relaxing state of mind, let's turn to problem solving to loosen you from the shackles of stress (or help you lift the restraining bar enough to let you grab that roller-coaster brake lever).

Problem-Solving Behaviors

The term "problem solving" may be a bit misleading here, as many stress-related problems can't be completely solved. For instance, if science class becomes more intense and burdensome, staying on top of it will help, but a different class subject may get taxing just as you work through science assignments. Or, if you and a friend are experiencing a conflict, you can work it out, but then the conflict could reemerge later or a different issue could crop up with another friend. Sometimes it can seem as if the problem is never-ending!

The goal of problem-solving behavior, therefore, is to *manage* stressful problems. In some cases, this may mean totally solving them, but in others, it may mean coping as well as you can to lower your stress.

The following coping strategies can help you manage stressful challenges and difficult situations that come your way.

1. Doing Instead of Stewing

Thoughts that come with stress, such as *I'll never be able to do this*, can sabotage your belief that you can get things done. Left to keep stewing, your thoughts may become even more twisted and discouraging—for example, *I can't seem to get motivated to do anything*. At such times, it may help if you can create any kind of spark for action. For example, if you're having a hard time starting that paper for English class, then perhaps accomplishing a quick, unrelated task, such as making your bed, will prime your motivation pump. This is better than waiting, perhaps days, for the "motivation fairy" to magically get you going ("I'll do it when I feel like it"—good luck with that!). "And if by chance you have a miserable day, you will come home to a bed that is made, that you made. And a made bed gives you encouragement that tomorrow will be better" (McRaven 2017).

Once you complete something smaller, even if it's unrelated, you may feel more like doing something bigger—like that English paper (did you think I'd forget to remind you?)! It's amazing how focusing on a quick and easily doable task can inspire you to approach a more challenging task. Success breeds success. Here are some quick ways you can help yourself get back on top of the responsibilities that lie ahead of you.

* Pick up those clothes on the floor and hang them in your closet.

* Vacuum your carpet (now that you've cleared a path on the floor).

* Clean out a desk drawer.

* Read or study for a little while.

* Make a to-do list.

Another thing you can do to get yourself going on that challenging task is just dip your toes in the water. Put fifteen minutes on the kitchen timer or that app on your phone, and get busy. If when the alarm goes off, you don't want to persist, then stop. Later, try another fifteen minutes.

2. Reempowering Yourself to Stay on Course

Once you're in action mode, you need to stay motivated to follow through in case you get stuck. You might get stuck in one of the following ways:

* You're studying, but then you get distracted and now you don't want to study anymore.

* You had planned to ask out your crush, but now you feel nervous and hesitant.

* You talked yourself into going to the gym yesterday, but now you feel hopelessly out of shape and don't want to go back.

* You're preparing to talk out a conflict with a friend but then become discouraged.

Just tell yourself these four magic words: "I'll do it anyway!" What's so cool about making "I'll do it anyway" your mind-set is that you don't have to "be ready" to approach stressful challenges. Let's break it down:

I'll: Puts you back in the driver's seat to claim responsibility for what you'll do.

Do: Redirects your thinking to the task or goal instead of continuing to lose sight of it.

It: Focuses you back on the specific task to be done.

Anyway: Creates a huge motivational influence because it acknowledges that you may feel strong resistance but will push through it to take action and get things done. (This inspires grit, which we'll further discuss in the next chapter.)

Even if you aren't completely feeling it, you can still do something that's in your best interests. Here's how you can apply this:

In Their Own Words

"I've learned that getting things done instead of moping around helps me feel better. If I even just clean out my backpack, I'm more motivated to do schoolwork. And if I still don't want to do it, I say to myself, *I'll do it anyway!* I get it out of the way and can do something fun afterward."
Nikia, age 15

3. Brainstorming to Make a Plan

When you're stressed out, you may feel that taking the time to plan your next move would waste precious time. Often when we face hard times, we just want to end the stress as soon as possible. This is totally understandable. But we often get ourselves even more stressed out when we rush in hastily to solve our problems. In addition, solutions that we haven't taken the time to think through might even make our problems worse.

When you feel like you don't know how to solve a stressful problem, you can try a strategy called brainstorming. This refers to the process of creatively reflecting on possible solutions to a problem—and not throwing any of them out until you've completely run out of ideas. The power of brainstorming comes from not judging your ideas prematurely. In fact, just allowing yourself to start to think about solving problems can give you a sense of hope.

Brainstorming involves:

* Coming up with ideas that might help with a problem

* Evaluating them as potential solutions to see what seems most helpful

* Trying them out in your mind to see how well they could work

* Picking the best idea to help you deal with the situation at hand

Let's take a look at how Troy used brainstorming to get past a huge disappointment that was very stressful to him.

Troy's Story

After not making his high-school basketball team, Troy said to his mother, "This serves me right, because I suck at basketball anyway!" At that moment, he wanted to stop playing basketball altogether. But then, as he reflected on the fun he had had in the past, he realized he would miss playing basketball if he gave it up. Troy turned to brainstorming to figure out what to do to get back into the game.

During his brainstorming session, he wrote down the following potential solutions. He also jotted down his thoughts below each one.

* Play video games related to basketball.

   Man, I really do love basketball! Even just playing this NBA video game is really fun. But I like being out there on the court even more.

* Have pickup games of basketball with friends.

   When me and my boys play, it is fun, but it would be cool to be on a real team for, like, a season, and I just wish there were real refs to enforce the rules.

• Join a laid-back community league that empha-
   sizes cooperation over competition.

   This is a cool league. So what if I didn't make the school team? I'm more at my skill level now, and I get more playing time here than I would in school games anyway.

4. Breaking Big Challenges into Small Parts

This strategy is similar to making a plan. At those times when you needed to start a big project for school, have you ever felt like your own worst enemy? Does the idea of looking for a part-time job seem over-whelming? When you think about filling out all those college applica-tions, do you start to feel smothered? Or maybe you haven't cleaned your room in a while because now there's just so much *stuff* and you can't possibly do it all.

We all can feel overwhelmed by complex tasks and activities. But they start to feel less impossible when we break them into steps. As automobile-manufacturing pioneer Henry Ford said, "Nothing is par-ticularly hard if you break it down into small jobs." (And building a car is one heck of a big job!)

Brandi's Story

Brandi was feeling overwhelmed with a written project for English class as the due date closed in fast. One night, as she struggled yet again to make a start, she explained her frustration in a social-media update: "I've read the book, and I know what I have to do, but I have, like, zero motivation, because I can't get going on it. Even just vaguely thinking about it gives me anxiety. My stomach does somersaults, and I get a lump in my throat. And that's how I feel when I'm not totally freaking out. When I actually think about how much I have to do to get this monster paper done, I start having a friggin' panic attack. Then I start thinking, I hate myself because I can never get things done!"

One of Brandi's friends replied with the suggestion that she challenge her all-or-nothing thinking (I can "never" get things done) by telling herself, I'm just feeling stuck at this time. Brandi listened and did. She then took some deep breaths and felt she was ready to take action and get going on her project. Stepping into problem-solving mode, Brandi made a list of past school projects that she had gotten done over the years. This gave her a boost of confidence.

Next, she calmly reflected on the book she was writing her paper about and realized she had some great ideas to capture. This renewed her enthusiasm for doing the assignment. She then broke her project down into phases; once she had done this, it felt far less overwhelming. Her problem-solving plan included the following steps:

- Develop an outline of my general ideas, which will become the framework of what I'll write about.

- Begin writing phases, then sentences, and then paragraphs based on my ideas.

- Come up with connections to tie the paragraphs together.

- Wrap up the assignment by writing a summary that links the ideas together.

By taking the time to break her project down into manageable parts, Brandi decreased her stress level while increasing her productivity.

5. Knowing When Less Is More

It's common to think that managing stress means doing more tasks or doing them faster. But sometimes, doing *less* can be better for your stress level and help you avoid going too far or wearing yourself out. Following are some examples of when less is more—more helpful, that is:

* Not over-studying when you're already adequately prepared for a test or presentation

* Realizing that you don't have to always be the one to keep your friends and peers entertained, especially if you're feeling pressure to do so

* Being aware of the extent to which you share personal information with acquaintances, to help prevent what you share from being taken out of context or misunderstood and distorted by others

* While being yourself, not coming on too strong when you're talking to your crush (e.g., if you tend to babble when you're nervous)

* Building self-confidence by going to a store or public place and smiling at, making eye contact, or saying hi to people, to help you feel more confident later in situations that tend to make you socially anxious

6. Being Assertive to Feel Better

Being assertive means speaking up for yourself. Assertive behavior helps you avoid bottling up your stress and exploding (or imploding) later. There's an important difference between being assertive and being aggressive. Being assertive means sticking up for your rights. Being aggressive may involve sticking up for your rights, but it disregards the rights of others. Also important is the difference between assertiveness and passive aggression. Passive-aggressive behaviors entail ignoring others (think giving someone the "silent treatment"), choosing inaction as a way to hurt others (think not following through on a promise), or pouting as a way to cause someone guilt.

Assertiveness can help with stressful struggles such as:

* Speaking up to a friend or someone in your family about something that bothers you

* Discussing a low grade you received on an assignment with your teacher

* Asking for time off from your job

* Telling your coach you want to take a shot at a different position

* Approaching a new peer you'd like to get to know better

Check out how being assertive helped Noreen, a high-school senior, feel less stressed out as a result of a very embarrassing situation.

Noreen's Story

Noreen had a mad crush on Moana, a girl in her class. Noreen texted Moana one day and asked if she'd like to go out on a date. Moana saw Noreen as a "sorta friend," but she kind of freaked out at being asked out by a girl, because so far she had only dated boys. Letting her reacting brain take over without pulling the brakes and hoping to cause a shock reaction like the one she felt (and also to get some input), she took a screenshot of the text message and sent it to a trusted friend—who then sent it to other people.

When Noreen heard about what had happened from a mutual friend, she felt humiliated and super-angry. At the same time, she really didn't want to lose Moana as a friend. She spoke to Moana at school about the text-sharing incident, and Moana tried to convince her that she was "just kidding around" and it was no big deal. When Noreen asked Moana if she was sorry for what she'd done, Moana said (with a hollow ring) that she was sorry but that Noreen was totally overreacting.

Noreen felt a little better for bringing it up, but, over the next few weeks, her feelings of embarrassment and anger returned. She decided to speak to Moana again, and this time, she was more assertive. She told Moana, "I know you said you thought it was no big deal, but I was still really hurt by the violation of my privacy." Moana, seeing that Noreen was self-confident and serious, finally conceded that what she had done was wrong. She apologized to Noreen in a more heartfelt way.

Try This! Practicing Being Assertive

Reflect on a time when you were bothered or offended but didn't speak up for yourself. Following are some examples of situations that might fit the bill.

- You lent a friend some money or a possession and didn't get it back.

- A friend promised to invite you to a party but never actually did.

- You didn't feel listened to by someone you were speaking with.

- You were directly teased in a way that upset you more than the other person realized.

- Someone made a hurtful comment about you on social media.

- Someone took your lunch seat in the cafeteria.

- A teacher was overly critical of your work.

- You were charged too much in error for an item at a store.

Now relive the situation in your mind and, this time, practice being assertive—by saying, "I felt _____ when you _____:" For example, "I felt
angry when you didn't keep your promise." As you do this, visualize yourself
looking straight at the person you're speaking with.

Afterward, reflect on the following questions:

How difficult was it for you to visualize yourself being assertive in this
situation?

What did practicing being assertive mean to you?

How can being assertive lower your stress level?

What would be the benefit of following up in real life with a situation
similar to the one you recalled in this activity?

Why do we tend to not be assertive at times? Is it due to fear of conflict? Or having low self-confidence? Or some other reason? By the
time you are through reading this book, you may be able to overcome
these issues better.

7. Asking for Help

Earlier in the chapter, we discussed reaching out when you feel
stressed out as a calming behavior to help you manage upsetting emotions. Now, however, I'm referring to not just sharing what you're going
through but seeking assistance to overcome a specific problem.

There's a common conception that we all should be able to solve
problems in our lives on our own. Although this sentiment *sounds*
noble, asking for help when you need it is a super-important skill. It
takes guts to ask for help, and doing so will not only make your life
feel better, but also help you be more successful in everything you do.
In addition, you can always repay the favor or pay it forward, which

will reward you with good feelings later. Check out how Dave, a high-school junior, learned the value of asking for help:

Dave's Story

Dave was agonizing and feeling super stressed out over his struggles with math. His math teacher was an intimidating lady who seemed to have no patience for students who were struggling to keep up. He had persistent thoughts of being a failure, which were especially triggered whenever he would try to do his math homework.

Once he got past labeling himself as a "total failure" and comparing himself with others who were better at math, he realized he was in over his head. He met with his school counselor to ask about dropping this tough math class. The counselor, however, had an alternative: Dave could be tutored by a senior who had taken the class the previous year. Dave agreed to try it, and the counselor put him in touch with a senior who was happy to help. In addition, when Dave's math teacher got wind of his troubles, she put aside some time once a week to give Dave one-on-one help. These personal meetings with her left him feeling less stressed and intimidated by her during class, which helped him absorb the information. Dave also listened to his parents' suggestion that he do his math homework earlier, in the afternoon, rather than putting it off until late in the evening. As a result of seeking help and advice from his counselor, his teacher, and his parents, Dave stopped beating himself up over his issues with math. In addition, it no longer took him so long to do his math homework. So, even with the tutoring and extra meetings with his teacher, he was able to enjoy more free time and keep up with his other classes better.

Try This! Knowing When It Helps to Get Help

Reflect on a difficult time or a situation that didn't turn out as well as you would've liked it to. Recall who else, if anyone, was around during the situation, what the situation meant to you, how you felt at the time, and how you felt after it was over.

Did getting help enter your mind in the midst of this situation?

Were you feeling resistant to seeking help? If so, why was that?

If you could do it all over again, how could seeking help have allowed you to handle the situation better?

Maybe there are times when you believe that asking someone for help could make a difficult situation worse. Unless you do ask, though, you can never know for sure, and you could be pleasantly surprised. Even if people can't help you themselves, they might offer valuable suggestions.

Putting It All Together

In this chapter, we discussed the importance of actions you can take to lower your stress by calming you down and giving you ways to manage the demands and problems of teenage life. We introduced skills such as brainstorming to help you figure out solutions to stressful situations.

Now you're ready to learn how positive psychology, your second roller-coaster brake lever, can help you as well.

PART 3

The Power of
Positive Psychology

chapter 6

Seeing Your Strengths, Optimism, and Grit

Both CBT and positive psychology emphasize that how we think influences how we feel about ourselves and our lives. Positive psychology, the topic of this chapter, is often referred to as the science of happiness. That's a pretty upbeat way to refer to a really cool concept!

The parts of positive psychology that we'll cover in this chapter include:

* Getting in touch with your strengths, which enable you to succeed

* Optimistic ways you can think and feel about yourself and your future

* Grit, which is the ability to persist when things are hard while developing the skills you need to accomplish challenging goals

What Is Positive Psychology *Really*?

Some people have misunderstandings about positive psychology, thinking that it means "just be happy" all the time and then your problems will magically disappear. They associate it with people who constantly smile, as though they don't have a worry in the world (no one like this truly exists). Some people even think that positive psychology involves memorizing special scripts that'll program their brains to be immune to the feelings of everyday stress. Let's put an end to the rumors and straighten out what positive psychology is and what it is not.

Positive Psychology Is...	Positive Psychology Is Not...
Seeing your inner strengths and talents	A set of self-brainwashing techniques to make you superior to others
Thinking about the challenges in your life in a more optimistic way to help you more fully engage and succeed in them	Thinking that happy, positive thoughts guarantee positive outcomes
Developing grit to persevere and find a way through setbacks and disappointments	Being able to completely eliminate adversity and prevent tough times
Getting "in the zone" and being in a state of joy while absorbed in what you're doing	Expecting activities to be automatically rewarding
Seeing that being more thankful helps you be happier	Assuming you'll automatically feel happier by having more good things in your life
Realizing that happiness takes practice	Training yourself to be effortlessly satisfied and happy all the time

In this chapter, we'll discuss knowing your strengths, having optimism, and gaining grit. In the next chapter, we'll cover the cool concept of flow and the importance of gratitude.

Let's now begin by discussing how knowing your strengths is a super-important gift you can give yourself, one that truly keeps on giving.

Standing Steady in Your Strengths

As a teen facing pressures to academically keep up, to socially fit in and thrive, to do sports or other activities, and maybe to get or keep a part-time job, you're already majorly busy. You may question the value of taking time out of your hectic schedule to focus on your strengths. But don't you tend to waste a lot of precious time and energy when you fill yourself with doubts that get in the way of getting things done?

Maybe you think that it seems self-absorbed to spend time reflecting on your strengths. Yet have you never admired someone who takes a healthy pride in their talents or accomplishments? And can you really think of any true downside to feeling a little clearer and better about who you are (and what you have to offer others) as a person?

Being aware of your strengths and valuing them is super-important, because it helps you feel happier and less stressed. Martin Seligman, who's considered the father of positive psychology, has observed that seeing our strengths and using them to help ourselves and others adds happiness and meaning to our lives.

Seeing your strengths doesn't mean ignoring your weaknesses. There's no doubt that there's value in being able to see your own struggles and limitations. The more you accept (without judgment) that there are areas in which you would benefit from improving, the more you can grow, the better you'll feel about yourself, and the more you can achieve in life. You may remember that, in the last chapter, we discussed the importance of asking for help when you need it. Well, admitting that there are some things you simply don't do as well as other people (at least, yet) can make it easier to seek and obtain help so that you don't get super stressed out. The key is not to criticize yourself for lacking the ability, skill, or time to do everything on your own.

When it comes to our weaknesses, though, we can really dwell on them and judge ourselves harshly for having them. Rick Hanson, a noted psychologist and author, once said that our brains are like Velcro for negative experiences and Teflon for positive ones (Bergeisen, 2010). (Teflon is that slick coating on nonstick pots and pans.) This is a colorful way of saying that people's natural inclination is to let negative stuff, including what we don't like about ourselves, really cling to our minds. As for our good qualities and accomplishments, we tend to forget them. We may think about them once in a while, but then they slide out of our consciousness as easily as fried eggs from a nonstick pan. This feeds a natural tendency for many of us to sell ourselves short, overlooking our positive qualities and how they can help boost us when we need to draw upon them.

Knowing and celebrating your strengths can go a long way toward helping you when you're facing stressful times. It can bolster your confidence and help you feel motivated to keep going when the going gets tough.

Check out how Sophia focused on her strengths to help her in a time of stress:

Sophia's Story

Sophia was struggling socially in school. Many of the girls around her were competing ruthlessly for popularity. They gossiped nonstop and, at times, were really mean to one another. One day, things really got stressful for Sophia when a girl whom she had just started to open up to was giving her the cold shoulder. That night she told another friend, Camila, that her life was going really badly, and she confided that, out of frustration, she had intentionally hurt herself by scratching her arm really hard with a hairbrush.

Camila, wanting to be supportive of Sophia and, knowing the dangers of self-harming behavior, sensed that it was important to get further help for her. So, the next day, she spoke to a school counselor. When Sophia was summoned to see the school counselor and learned the reason why, she was initially disappointed in Camila. I can't believe she went behind my back. She's just like the other girls, Sophia fumed.

Fortunately, her school counselor, while being a patient and supportive listener, helped Sophia see that Camila was a true friend for caring about her. To decelerate her roller coaster of stress, the school counselor encouraged Sophia to consider her own strengths that she had lost sight of, as well as helped her identify some strengths she didn't know she possessed. Together, Sophia and her counselor made a list of her strengths:

- Authentic and open with others

- Kind

- Committed and loyal

- Creative

- Humorous

- Nonjudgmental

Sophia found it really cool that making this list helped her see her worth. It kind of freed her from all the pressures she'd been feeling, because no matter what anyone—such as the gossipy girls in her grade—said or did, she felt okay about herself as a person with many good qualities and as a loyal, caring friend to a lucky few.

Sophia had had little sense of her own strengths, but her school counselor did a great job helping her notice them. Her story teaches us a valuable lesson that seeing the good that others see in us can help us rediscover our own value when we're struggling with our self-worth.

The following activity will help you see your strengths through the eyes of the important people in your life. Once you allow yourself to reflect on the strengths others see in you, you'll likely start to perceive other strengths you possess. Your stream of personal strengths may start with just a trickle, but if you can be a little patient, then it may begin to flow more abundantly with good things about you.

Try This! Eyeing Your Strengths Through Others

Ask someone you feel close to and trust (like a friend, a family member, or a teacher) what he or she values about you. If you're not comfortable asking for this feedback at this time, then just reflect on what positive qualities others have complimented you on or seem to value in you.

Consider the following questions to help you get in touch with the strengths that others see in you.

What have people told you that you're good at doing?

What personality characteristics and values of yours have people told you that they appreciate?

When you receive compliments, how do you feel?

What things do you do that make people smile?

How have you felt when you've supported friends or family members to see their own strengths, at times when they were struggling and perhaps had lost sight of them?

What's one thing you value about yourself whether others see it or not?

Afterward, reflect on how you felt when going through the above questions. Can reflecting on the strengths and virtues that others see in you help you see them in yourself? If you were feeling stressed at the start of this activity, did your mood improve once you started identifying your strengths?

The more you value yourself, the less likely it is that you'll feel helpless when facing stressful situations—because you'll know that you can rely on your strengths and other good qualities to see you through hard times. Now let's turn to optimism, which is another important concept in positive psychology that can help you manage stress.

Optimism

Optimism means having hope that things will turn out well, while pessimism refers to believing that the future is bound to be negative. Let's first discuss pessimism to help you appreciate optimism, which is the opposite of it. Do you ever feel that there's too much negative energy coming from you or others? Do a lot of your friends gripe or groan about schoolwork, the frequent demands of extracurricular activities, and almost everything? Do you ever complain to them, too, because all the complaining around you feels infectious?

Can you see how focusing on negative energy within or around you stresses you out? In contrast, do you notice yourself feeling more upbeat when you expect good things to happen? How does this compare with how you feel when you think bad things are coming your way? How about your friends' outlooks? Would you rather hang out with your friends if they're being all gloom and doom or if they seem more upbeat and hopeful?

You've likely heard the expression, "Is the glass half empty or half full?" This refers to being able to see stressful situations, and the world in general, in either a pessimistic or an optimistic manner. Pessimists are those who see the glass as half empty, whereas optimists see it as half full. Pessimists tend to think more about falling short or failing in the face of challenges, while optimists see themselves as conquering those challenges—perhaps not right away, but eventually.

A huge difference between pessimists and optimists is in how they think in times of stress and adversity. When things don't go well, pessimists tend to blame themselves and tend to see their problems as permanent. Let's say you have a pessimistic view. If you do poorly on a test, you might say, "I just can't learn this subject." This implies there's something wrong with you and that you don't measure up. Thinking this way is likely to stress you out, because it makes you feel powerless. Your defeat (in this case, your failure to do well on the test) gradually becomes tied to how you view yourself, as someone who can't succeed.

Optimists, on the other hand, are hopeful. When things don't go well, they focus on what they can do to try to make things go better the next time around. Optimists understand that they're never really defeated, because they can develop their abilities in many ways that might help them reach their goals. So, as an optimist, if you fail a test, you might say something like, "I'll approach studying this subject in a different way, and I'll do better on the next test." The power of optimism is well expressed in a quotation often attributed to philosopher and psychologist William James (1842–1910): "Pessimism leads to weakness, optimism to power."

Thinking optimistically calms down your reacting brain, and it keeps the amount of cortisol released in your body more stable. Less cortisol, as you may remember from part 1, means feeling less stress, which is a really good thing!

Do you remember the diagram in chapter 5 showing the cycle of positive thoughts, feelings, and behaviors? This applies to the power of being optimistic. Expecting good things to happen (generating positive thoughts) will influence you to feel and behave in ways that'll help you achieve better outcomes when you face challenges.

You may think that you're simply a natural pessimist, and optimism is something that only other people can do. Although it's true that some people are wired to be more optimistic than others, it's a skill that anyone can learn. Martin Seligman, whom we mentioned above, showed through his research that we can learn to be more optimistic by training ourselves to do so (Holland 2015)!

Below are two activities to help you practice becoming more optimistic.

Try This! Flipping to the Upside

Reflect on a current situation that you don't believe will turn out as well as you'd like it to. What are the beliefs that go along with seeing this situation in a negative light? Take a moment to identify the feelings and bodily reactions that you're experiencing now or that you experience whenever the situation seems the worst. Then ask yourself the following questions:

> What messages from my past or from others are leading to my pessimistic view of this situation? (Consider those stubborn, lingering sound bites floating in your mind, such as "He's out of your league," "There's no way you'll make the varsity team," "No offense, but trust me, applying to that college will be a waste of your time," or "Just saying—they really didn't seem interested in what you were talking about.")

> Why else have I been buying into the idea that things won't go as well as I'd like them to?

> What would it actually take for this situation to go well for me?

What unique strengths and values have I learned that I possess and that I can use to increase the chances of things turning out well?

Now you're beginning to think about things more optimistically! Has your view of the stressful situation changed for the better? If so, take a minute to go through the same process whenever you sense that you're being too pessimistic or your reacting brain is telling you that things are hopeless. Flipping to the upside can ease your stressed-out mind and spur you to take positive actions to get through the situation just fine.

Now let's shift to an activity (developed by researcher Laura King and popularized by Sonja Lyubomirsky) that focuses the power of optimism by having you look at your long-term success and happiness to help you feel better now. You can use it any time you feel down about your life in general. In doing so, you'll be training your brain to take a more optimistic view of your overall future!

Try This! Seeing Your Best Self Through Time

Close your eyes, and think about your life right now. Then slowly start to fast-forward. Imagine that everything is going as well as it could be in the next few months—academically, socially, in your personal life, and in your job, if you have one. What have you accomplished, and what are you doing? Visualize your best possible life six months from now, in all that detail. Have you thought of everything? Good.

Now visualize your best possible life one year from now. You've worked to overcome your challenges and are making progress. You're a year older, a year wiser, a year closer to your long-term goals.

Then imagine your best possible life five years from now. You've had a lot of successes. What does your family or romantic life look like, and how are you keeping your relationships strong? What are you studying in college, or to what exciting places is your career taking you?

In what ways are you already on the road to creating this bright future for yourself?

Does focusing on a positive future help lift your mood in the present?

Does reflecting on being in these great future scenarios inspire you to take any particular actions to achieve what you're visualizing?

Does focusing on a positive image of your future self help you feel less stressed?

Here's what other teens have said about how positive psychology helped them feel better about themselves and helped them manage their stress.

In Their Own Words

"My older sister told me I was being super-negative and it was annoying her. I guess she learned about positive psychology in a class and told me it can help me to feel encouraged by knowing there are possibilities. So I tried looking for the good stuff in my life instead of just focusing on negative things that could happen to me." **Bruce, age 13**

"I was getting *way* too negative in my head by focusing on all the complaining from a few of my friends. All they were talking about was lousy teachers and friend drama. But then I realized I could choose to look at things more positively." **Katie, age 15**

"I really thought I was going to fail English. But when I met with my teacher, she helped me see that even though I had more work to do on my written assignment, I was getting much closer to having it done compared to a week ago. This gave me hope." **Marina, age 17**

You may recall, as mentioned in chapter 3, that optimists tend to take more risks than pessimists. With this in mind, it's important to realize that seeing your life in an overly optimistic way can have downfalls, which could involve either overestimating your abilities or underestimating the risks involved in certain activities. (Given that you're reading this book about surviving stress, however, chances are that you're not prone to unrealistic optimism.) In short, optimism can help you feel better about yourself and achieve your goals, but it can't replace the hard work and sensible precautions it'll take to keep you on the best course.

Now that you've learned the value of seeing your strengths, and you've had a taste of what optimism can do for you, let's talk about grit.

Gaining Grit

Stressful, negative thoughts can pound away at you, leaving you feeling almost like you've been repeatedly walloped by a professional fighter. They can bruise your ego and discourage you from pursuing your goals. But when you get going with grit, you'll feel an unwavering commitment to persevere.

Grit is the unswerving commitment to learning the best ways to reach your goals even when doing so doesn't feel gratifying. When you become a gritty person, you don't let setbacks and failures stop you from pursuing what you're striving for. You continue to have passion and to practice whatever you need to learn to be successful. In other words, when it comes to dealing with difficult challenges, you might feel dejected now and again, but you refuse to completely lose heart.

According to Angela Duckworth (quoted in Holland 2015), grit comes from staying with goal-oriented tasks (doing things that will *get* you somewhere) even when they start to feel boring or didn't give you much sense of reward in the first place (sometimes this may apply to uninteresting schoolwork, a grueling sports practice, or a job that doesn't suit you). Duckworth points out that grit is all about continuing to pursue an objective, no matter what challenges arise. Let's look at four things you can do to instill yourself with grit:

* Have a sense of purpose.

* Put in the time and effort required.

* Focus on your goal, not on feeling good right now.

* Look past setbacks.

If you can do these things in any single area of your life, even to achieve a short-term goal, you'll be geared up with grit for future endeavors. Let's take a look at each one.

Having a Sense of Purpose

There's a popular phrase in military circles that starts in boot camp: "Embrace the suck." This refers to completing a task that feels boring or pointless, such as peeling potatoes for the mess hall or filling sandbags to construct barriers for use in training exercises. The point is that, yes, it sucks, but you (as a military service member) can choose to do it proudly because every job, regardless of how small or tedious, is one that relates to something you value: serving your country.

If, like an army recruit, you can find some purpose behind doing a task you don't want to do, it can propel you to any goal. You may think, for example, *Who cares about geometry? I probably won't use it in the real world.* But if you might like to design video games, to build robots, or to invent electronic gadgets, just think about how video-game graphics and visual-recognition software programs rely on concepts in geometry.

The more you see your efforts, whatever they are, as part of something that is or could be valuable to you, the grittier you'll become when you trudge through challenging tasks. One way to help you focus with a sense of purpose is to see these tasks not as things you "have to do" but as things that can help you earn the patience and persistence to achieve your dreams. Because, as the saying goes, nothing worth having comes easily. And "the little things in life matter. If you can't do the little things right, you'll never be able to do the big things right" (McRaven 2017).

Putting In the Time and Effort

Grit is about persevering when you'd rather be doing something else. It's about pushing your limits and expanding your capabilities. There's just no other way to get really good at something. Malcolm Gladwell, in his book entitled *Outliers: The Story of Success* (2008), revealed that many star athletes, billionaires, famous musicians, and other kinds of highly successful people spent seemingly endless time and energy on honing their skills. According to Gladwell's findings, these extremely talented people spend *ten thousand hours* practicing to obtain their amazing achievements. For many, this means practicing twenty hours a week, for ten years. That's some serious grit!

Even Mozart wasn't born a great piano player. It took dedication, discipline, and training. Imagine if the first time he sat at a piano bench, he had played a few notes and decided that he was no good. The same goes for how athletes progress into professional sports. The major-league baseball players that appear on the field in those big fancy stadiums have rich backstories of ups and downs from when they played on smaller-level farm teams that paved the way for them to get to the big leagues. So, don't let the fact that you're not an instant pro turn you off or prevent you from getting better. Skills are cultivated, not congenital. You have to crawl before you can walk!

Rock climber Alex Honnold provides a wonderful example of this aspect of grit. Honnold, the first and only person ever to scale the granite monolith known as El Capitan, in California's Yosemite National Park, without using ropes(!) (as seen in the documentary film *Free Solo*), has said:

> I was never, like, a bad climber [as a kid], but I was never a great climber, either… There were a lot of other climbers who were much, much stronger than me, who started as kids and were, like, instantly freakishly strong—like they just have a natural gift. And that was never me. I just loved climbing, and I've been climbing all the time ever since, so I've naturally gotten better at it, but I've never been gifted. (quoted in Munchies, 2015)

This just goes to show you that even those who are truly the best at what they do don't necessarily feel like they're the best. You don't have to feel like you're the best either, but you do have to practice if you want to be really good.

Focusing on Your Goal, Not on Feeling Good Right Now

A big part of grit is being able to focus on how good you'll feel *after* doing something difficult. This is known as "delaying gratification." Too often, when faced with what looks like a challenging situation, many teens choose the path that seems easiest or the one that'll give them a good feeling the fastest. So, rather than writing that paper for school, practicing their musical instrument, or rehearsing lines for the play, they binge-watch a television show, play video games, or hang out with friends, because it feels more enjoyable. But if they keep ditching their "work," you can imagine how that decision will come back to bite them when they get a bad grade, flub their way through the recital, or freeze up onstage. So just know that, by focusing on the satisfaction you'll gain from being persistent in meeting a challenge, the less stressed out you'll be in the end. This can help you get past the temporary discomfort of something you don't want to do. And even if you don't meet your goal, knowing that you've given it your best will feel far more satisfying than knowing you gave up on an important quest.

Looking Past Setbacks

Have you ever noticed how people love to root for the underdog in sports? Do you also value seeing people triumph after facing difficult times? Many folks admire the story of Thomas Edison, who tried and failed a whole lot in his attempt to invent the incandescent light bulb. He's quoted as having said, prior to his success: "I have not failed. I've just found 10,000 ways that won't work." As another cool inspiring example of grit, professional surfer Bethany Hamilton started riding waves when she was just a child. At thirteen, she lost her left arm to a shark. But she was soon back on her surfboard and went on to take first place in the Explorer Women's Division of the NSSA National Championships (Jacques 2013).

Try This! Seeing Others' Grit to Find Yours

Think about someone famous who you look up to. It might be a singer, an actor, an athlete, or the president of a wildly successful tech company. Now imagine the hard work and setbacks that person had to overcome to get where they are today. You might actually look up biographical information online and search for information in their background or history that proves they didn't have an easy time. You're bound to find some clues, at the least.

As a variation on this activity, think of a favorite movie hero or an inspiring fictional character and remind yourself of the many hurdles and battles they faced almost from the very beginning.

Does seeing grit in this famous person inspire you to move past your own reluctance to strive for new goals, even though you could fail to achieve them?

Can you see from the story of this person's struggles and success that initial reluctance to confront a challenge can deprive you of finding a way to achieve the "impossible"?

Can you use the knowledge that this person must have felt similar to the way you feel at times to help you not feel so alone or to get back up when life knocks you down?

How does grit build your sense of confidence?

What struggles have you weathered or would you now endure realizing that doing so will make you stronger, just as it did for this person you admire?

Remember this part of you that roots for others to triumph, and draw on this gritty energy when facing difficult challenges that lie ahead.

There's an ancient Japanese proverb: "Fall down seven times, stand up eight." This refers to the ability to bounce back when you face hard times. The fact is that setbacks will be a part of your journey, but you can still cheer yourself onward and maybe try a different approach.

You can stay positive about what you're striving for even when you struggle. Try to reframe setbacks as learning experiences. When things get tough, it's easy to get smothered with self-doubts, such as "What if I fail?" Just tune back in to your sense of purpose to keep yourself focused on your goal. Concentrate on what you *can* do to keep moving toward what you desire.

The good news about grit is that you don't have to climb a mountain (like Alex Honnold) to develop it. Check out Cindy and Jose's stories to get a sense of how these two teens found grit on the ground level.

Cindy's Story

When Cindy saw a karate demonstration at an assembly at her middle school, it inspired her to learn karate. Her parents supported the idea, and she began taking lessons from the same karate studio that had done the demonstration at her school.

Cindy was about fifteen pounds overweight, and she found the classes to be physically more taxing than she had anticipated. She stayed with the karate instruction for a year and got promoted to yellow belt, but then she sprained her shoulder when sparring with a partner. This injury upset her, because she feared that it would slow her progress to the next belt. The doctor told her that she'd have to lay off punches and other strenuous arm movements for up to six months. Motivated by her commitment and sense of purpose, she still went to karate class (with the doctor's approval) but focused on her kicks instead of her punches. It took a long time for her injury to heal so that she could get back to full participation and pursuing her goal of advancing through the ranks, but she stuck with it. She ended up getting her black belt just before leaving for college (one year later than planned) yet was proud about pursuing her goal in spite of her physical challenges and the setback from her injury.

Jose's Story

Jose, age fourteen, was hoping to enroll in an elite private high school specializing in STEM. Unfortunately, his parents' flooring business took a major downturn after a big competitor moved into the area. When his parents told him that they wouldn't be able to afford the school of his choice, Jose was very disappointed.

Jose told himself after a while that he had to at least try to find a way to go to the STEM school. He took a job on weekends at a fast-food restaurant. It wasn't the best gig, but his purpose wasn't to have fun or to get a great learning experience—it was to make as much money as he could to contribute toward his goal. Yet whatever he made working part-time would clearly not be enough to cover the cost of the private school tuition, so Jose requested a meeting with the headmaster for him and his parents.

The headmaster was impressed with Jose's determination and encouraged him to apply for scholarships and seek other financial aid. Jose's strengths were in math and science, but he struggled with writing, so the prospect of submitting essays (as required for

many scholarships) was daunting. But he sought out help from his
English teacher at his current school and kept working on them.
On weekends, Jose split his time between working on his essays and
working at the restaurant. He eventually received three scholarships,
allowing him to attend the private school.

In order to embrace grit for your future, it helps to take a close look at any past patterns of giving up on your goals and to commit to not repeating those patterns. Check out the following exercise to learn about the thoughts and feelings that may have led you to fall short on past opportunities and goals.

Try This! Letting Go of Giving Up

Think about your past accomplishments that you're proud of. Now reflect on a goal you wanted to achieve but then became discouraged and gave up on. Get in touch with what was going on within you and around you when this challenge wasn't met. Now consider the questions below. (If you can't come up with a time you gave up on a goal, then do this exercise with a family member and listen to what they have to say.)

Did you feel a true sense of purpose in pursuing that goal?

If you abandoned your efforts fairly soon, what thoughts and feelings led you to do so?

If you put in a considerable amount of effort, what discouraged you from continuing to do so? Did you lose your sense of purpose?

Looking back, did you overestimate or underestimate the amount of effort that was necessary to reach your goal?

Keep believing in your efforts, and you'll be more likely to stick with your future goals.

Once you learn to overcome a few stressful challenges, you'll feel stronger and will be able to persevere more often, even if there's a chance you'll fail. That's the power of grit for you! The only way to become successful at anything is to try, and continuing to try new things is essential to your personal growth. In the 1990s, superstar Michael Jordan, who had retired from basketball, switched to baseball as a way to stay active in professional sports. It turned out he wasn't that great at it, but he did value his efforts to broaden his experience in a fun way. As he said in his book, "I can accept failure, everyone fails at something. But I can't accept not trying" (Jordan 1994). This is an inspirational message for anyone who aspires to greater heights or grander dreams.

Check out the following activity to help you get gritty in facing challenges in your life.

Try This! Gritting Out Future Challenges

Think about something you would like to do even though it would be challenging and perhaps difficult. Reflect on what others have said or why you believe this undertaking would be a tough one. Think about how putting in the required time and effort may feel dull and even taxing. For example, if you would like to have a more muscular physique, think about how by lifting weights you will pay some temporary dues of feeling tired and sore along the way.

What are you telling yourself that's hindering you from trying to reach this goal?

If you fail to reach this goal, what's the worst that could happen?

What goals have you, in the past, fallen short of at first but then went on to achieve?

How does struggling to succeed help you have more confidence in yourself once you achieve your goal? Does earning a reward through hard work feel better than just being handed it on a plate?

Putting It All Together

In this chapter, we looked at the sense of empowerment you can gain by focusing on your strengths, having an optimistic outlook, and developing grit. These three elements of positive psychology can foster a sense of inner strength, because they'll give you confidence in who you are as a person and what you can do.

In the next chapter, we'll focus on the concept of flow—which is about the joy you get from being in the moment—and the power of gratitude.

chapter 7

Finding Flow and Gaining Gratitude

In this chapter, we'll discuss two more powerful stress-lowering tools from positive psychology: flow and gratitude. Flow occurs when you're totally absorbed in doing something interesting and challenging. It lowers your stress because it shifts you away from thoughts and feelings that upset you. Gratitude takes you to an awesome, stress-releasing emotional state as well. When you focus on appreciating and reflecting on great times and experiences in your life, you won't feel as much anxiety. Both flow and gratitude create a sense of comfort and happiness, very much the opposite of the feelings of worry, frustration, and anger that come along for the ride when you're soaring along on the roller coaster of stress.

You'll likely find it very helpful to use flow and gratitude to help to quiet your mind when you feel unable to relax because your mind is dwelling on past setbacks or is filled with insecure thoughts and feelings. At times like these, when you're filled with self-doubts, flow and gratitude can reboot your brain and help you gather yourself back together. Seeing your strengths, becoming optimistic, and gaining grit, which you learned about in the last chapter, can give you the mental traction to break free and take action. Flow and gratitude, on the other hand, can help you keep a healthy, positive perspective to accept and improve a troubling situation or a seemingly hopeless one.

For example, you just went on a great first date but haven't heard back from that special person in two days. You keep wondering why they haven't called yet, obsessing about whether they like you, and wanting to pick up the phone, even though your friends all tell you that you need to wait at least another day so that you don't seem too thirsty. Rather than spending that whole day being unhappy, or even fighting off feeling desperate, you can enjoy what your life has to offer. It's about taming your desire for things to be different than they are and also making good use of your time when things are going well. Allowing yourself to feel grateful when she or he calls, for example, will enhance your positive feelings even further.

Going with the Flow

Flow is all about intense focus. Think for a minute about how being distracted often increases your stress, especially when your thoughts wander into a counterproductive direction. It's commonly estimated that our brains generate roughly fifty thoughts per minute, which adds up to about fifty to seventy thousand thoughts per day. With this being the case, you can see how easy it is for your mind to wander! As you know, sometimes those thoughts are stressful ones, or even thoughts about stress—for example, worrying that you're too stressed out! You can use your first brake lever, your CBT skills, to dispute those unhelpful, counterproductive thoughts that are in the mix. And as a part of your second brake lever, positive psychology, by getting into flow you'll be sharply focused only on what you're doing in the present moment. This will lead those stressful thoughts right out of your mind for a while.

People describe flow as an almost magical feeling. Mihaly Csikszentmihalyi, the psychologist who popularized the concept, described it as occurring when you push your limits to achieve a goal. But flow can occur in everyday situations as well. For example, if you're in a stimulating conversation with friends, and you're really enjoying and focused on the topic at hand, it can become a flow experience. Flow may also come to you when you're on the basketball court or soccer field, when you're strumming your guitar, or when you're drawing on your sketchpad.

If you ask your friends about flow, they may describe it happening for them when they lift weights, practice their dance moves, do marching-band routines, or engage in a great topic on the debate team. By following your interests, you can experience it too. You might find your flow when reading a really interesting book, watching an engrossing movie, surfing social media, or playing a video game. In short, you can enter flow by doing anything in which you're highly immersed in an experience that offers some sort of continuous challenge to your mind and/or body. (I recommend you don't spend all your time doing your number-one favorite thing, whether it's video games or jogging— balance is healthy, so try to have a mix of rewarding experiences!)

So how can you tell if you're in flow? You can tell that you've moved into flow when the following things are going on.

You lose awareness of time. Feeling short on time is a leading cause of stress. Just think of that morning madness you may feel after waking up late and trying to still get to school on time. Or how about those homework and school project deadlines that always seem to come too soon? Sometimes just feeling anxious can also lead you to feel like time's running out. For example, think about how time seems to be closing in super-fast if you're trying to get up the guts to ask someone you *really* like to go to a dance. On the other hand, being stuck with too much time on your hands can be stressful too. You might wish you were somewhere else, or you might feel antsy. Boredom can be uncomfortable, especially when time slows to a crawl!

In contrast to feeling stressed about things moving too fast or too slow, being in flow leaves you feeling disconnected from time—in a really cool way. Have you ever been so into doing something that you lost track of time? Maybe this happened when you were drawing a picture, playing a sport, or jamming on a musical instrument. Perhaps you lost a sense of time when hiking on an enjoyable yet challenging trail. By learning to get into flow, you'll disconnect from the stress of time and other demands by intently focusing on something pleasurable that requires your full attention in the moment.

You're all in. When doing many everyday things, like killing time before homeroom or walking to class, you probably feel like you're just going through the motions. In instances like these, you either don't feel as though what you're doing is important or are just not interested. In short, your mind is on something else. When you're in flow, it's the complete opposite: you feel that what you're doing *is* important, and your interest is totally dialed in!

Have you ever felt like you didn't want to stop focusing on what you were doing, because you were completely immersed in it? Maybe you were working on a project for school that really meant a lot to you, and you were crushing it. Or perhaps you were playing a sport, and you were really "in the zone." Have you ever been hungry or tired but then started to do something you like and gotten so involved in it that your desire for food or sleep seemed to disappear? Yep, there are times when flow can even distract you from being "hangry"! When an experience or activity has you so engrossed that you lose sight of things going on around you, or the physical sensations within you, then you're likely in flow.

You feel motivated and super-focused. Do you ever feel like you just can't get into doing something, even though you really want to? For example, you're trying to understand your textbook, but you end up reading the same paragraph over and over and very little of it seeps into your mind. You're motivated, and you're working hard, but you just can't get the hang of it. You can't seem to find your stride. This is to say that flow won't always come to you. But sometimes, if you consciously and diligently focus on a task, you'll know you're in flow when the task starts to seem almost too easy. That "I got this" feeling is what comes from being totally tuned in and mindfully doing all you can to achieve a goal.

Check out how Victor discovered flow and the value he found in it for lowering his stress in the mornings before going to school.

Victor's Story

Victor was super-stoked to be in his last year of high school. Once he started getting accepted to colleges, however, his mind began to race with stressful thoughts related to future uncertainties. His main source of stress was regarding his deep commitment to his girlfriend, Louisa, who was a junior at his school. His top-choice colleges were more than three hours' drive away, and he was upset about the possibility of a long-distance relationship with Louisa not working out.

Wanting to feel more in control of his life, Victor thought about getting into better physical shape. He decided to wake up early each morning and go for a run before showering. The first day, he ran a mile, and it took him thirteen minutes. He decided to set a goal that would challenge him: to run three miles in under twenty-five minutes. While his morning runs required more physical exertion than he was used to, he began to find them really calming. As he diligently pursued his goal, he focused on his bodily movements when running, and this often gave him flow experiences. He felt a sense of dedication to his new pursuit and cherished each morning run as an opportunity to not be wrapped up in his own thoughts. After each run, he felt a sense of triumph at being that much closer to his goal, which he reached within three months. And focusing on something he could totally control—his fitness goal—helped him be more at peace with the things he might not be able to control, such as the potential fate of his relationship with Louisa.

Here's what Victor and some other teens say about discovering flow:

In Their Own Words

"I was, at first, just thinking of running as something I needed to do to feel better. But my fourth time out was really special, because it was the first time I noticed this thing called flow happen. Man, I just felt myself get totally into the run. I was so chill, it was amazing. Like, my whole body and my head was into what I was doing, and nothing else mattered." **Victor, age 18**

"My swim coach told me about getting into flow when we train for meets. I wasn't sure what he meant, but this one practice I was totally in the zone. I nailed it on my backstroke and got a new PR [personal record]." **Janice, age 16**

"My mom says when she goes fishing it's about forgetting everything. So, this one time I went with her to check it out, and it was awesome. I thought I'd be bored, but it was really cool to be out there and feel relaxed. I lost track of everything—but in a good way." **Kevin, age 14**

"I was drawing a portrait of my sister from a picture we took on vacation. I got really focused and felt really into it when I was drawing her." **Lisa, age 13**

As you can see, to enter into flow you don't have to climb a mountain or even run a mile. You can experience flow by having a stimulating conversation with friends about something you're totally into, such as music, art, or movies.

Check out the following activity to help build your awareness of when you've been in flow so that you can really feel it going forward.

Try This! Exploring Your Flow Experiences

Recall those activities you've been super-into, felt really motivated about, and lost yourself in. To help you discover and reflect on times you've been in flow, think of your areas of interest and your most pleasurable experiences involving them. Now ask yourself the following questions:

What engaging things have you done during which you were unaware of the passage of time?

What things and situations have kept you really absorbed, leaving you feeling disconnected from outside pressures and demands?

What things give you big-time satisfaction because you feel good about having done them?

How does actively being engaged in fun, meaningful activities impact your stress level?

Now that you're starting to recognize the times that you've been in flow, use that knowledge to help you get into flow the next time you're feeling stressed.

There will be times, however, when your options are limited or for some reason you can't do your favorite flow activity (for example, you lost a privilege, you're slammed with homework, the weather's bad, or you're away from home). Even if that's the case, you can turn an activity that has never created flow into one that will, for a little while. Even the simple act of walking can give you a flow experience, if you do it deliberately and really focus on what's special about it. Let's now have you try to go with the flow by doing this ordinary, everyday activity. As you may see, by placing all your attention on walking, just like anything else you might do, you can transform this often mindless and forgettable experience into a flow state.

Try This! Getting into Flow One Step at a Time

Find a setting where you feel inspired to walk. Where you wish to do some walking today may be different from where you want to try it next time, and that's okay. Maybe today you're in an outdoor park mood, and next time you'll want to do it with more privacy in your room or even your basement. Wherever you choose to walk, please turn off or refrain from using personal electronic devices for this activity.

As you head toward the location you've decided on for this activity, mindfully pay special attention to your own movements and to your surroundings (such as the surrounding trees). You can also focus on something you see, hear, or even smell. (It's likely that focusing this special way initially or when doing the walking won't come easily to you, so just please assure yourself that this is part of being in flow. It helps you direct your awareness to the present moment, which will pay off over time—meaning that the more you practice doing this activity, the more likely you'll get into "the zone" or flow.)

When you're ready to start the activity, stand still for a moment. Gently tell yourself that whatever's currently on your mind or even stressing you out can be put on hold for a few minutes. Take a few deep breaths, doing the best you can to focus all your attention on the present.

Intensely engage your attention on beginning to walk. Notice your feet, legs, and full body as you move along in a deliberate manner, while being in the moment. You can fix your gaze on an object in front of you or simply gaze ahead without any specific goal other than allowing yourself to advance forward.

Continue slowly walking for ten steps, and then take ten quickly paced steps. Then take ten more slow and ten more fast steps. If you wish to do all of your steps slowly, that's okay too. The main emphasis is not your speed but rather walking without being on autopilot, as we all so often are. By feeling challenged to experience yourself walking with as much attention as possible, you're now flowing into a more heightened sense of awareness of what's going on inside and around you.

Keep a sense of purpose by paying close attention to your movements. Notice your intention as you walk, particularly the sensations in your feet as they make contact with the ground and then come up again and how your body feels in the process as well. You can let your steps carry you in a straight line, a circle, or whatever comes naturally.

Stay tuned in to the present moment by focusing on your breath, while continuing to note how your weight shifts as you maintain your focus on putting one foot in front of the other. *Follow what feels good to you in terms of the duration of this activity. If completing the four sets of ten steps has given you that sense of absorbed focus while noticing the experience of walking in a way you haven't before, then you can end the activity.* If you want to keep going with the flow, continue the alternating mindful steps for another cycle of ten and ten. If you just aren't feeling flow when you do this exercise, don't feel discouraged. Just try this activity again later a couple of times. Keep an open mind as you do it, and you'll likely feel that absorbed, challenged feeling of flow in one of your next mindful walking sessions.

Afterward, do a flow check to see how this experience felt for you.

Did you briefly lose track of time or have it fade a bit from your awareness?

Can you see how changing up your walking experience by challenging yourself to note what's going on around you, inside you, and below you takes your mind away from stressful thoughts and to a calmer place that comes from increased awareness?

Did you feel engaged with a sense of purpose?

Could you notice how calling upon your focus cleared your mind of other thoughts, including stressful ones?

As this simple activity illustrates, opportunities to get into flow are readily available if you let yourself go there, even if just by foot.

When you take the time to really focus on your body in motion, rather than your thoughts or the world around you, you see that it truly is an amazing machine. Even walking involves a surprising amount of moving parts and complex coordination. You might sometimes wish your body was different, but it gets you from place to place and does a lot more, too. Sadly, we often take our bodies and other incredible gifts in our lives for granted. This brings us to being grateful for what you have—rather than focusing, as you're probably used to, on what you don't like about it or what you don't have.

Gratitude

We tend to overthink what we want in life or to preoccupy ourselves with seeking out new and exciting things. When we look around our homes, or even look in the mirror, we often focus on what we seem to lack. Or we imagine that having something "better" would improve our lives in some way. For example, you might glance at your old video-game console and wish you had the latest Xbox instead. You might glimpse your reflection and wish you had clearer skin or more manageable hair. When we think about all the things we don't possess, it can understandably leave us feeling empty. If we, instead, pause to reflect on and value all the things we already have in our lives, we feel more content.

Unfortunately, it's easy to lose sight of the contentment that can come from appreciating what we have at the present time. Gratitude can feel hard to hold on to for long, given that our consumer culture propels us to yearn for what we see around us, including all the trappings of those happy, happy people on social media. Many of us are fooled into thinking our lives will feel more complete if only we have more—more friends, more money, a bigger bedroom, a newer mobile device—but that mind-set is so hard to shake that nothing makes us happy for very long. Because no matter how much you have, you can always have more. But believe it or not, your life is already full of good stuff. And the way to be happy is to appreciate the things you have, whether that's a little or a lot.

Focusing on the things in your life that you're grateful for feels good, because it relieves the stress of striving to have more. It promotes a sense of peace when you value the good stuff in your life. Gratitude also moves you away from unfavorably comparing yourself with others. Theodore Roosevelt, our twenty-sixth president, said, "Comparison is the thief of joy." What this means is that unfavorably comparing your-self with others (which is one of the types of distorted negative think-ing we mentioned in chapter 3) leaves you feeling unhappy. Looking at your life all on its own, on the other hand, promotes a sense of fulfill-ment and joy.

Research shows that gratitude lowers our stress levels. When we think about the good stuff that we have in our lives and reflect on it with appreciation, the thinking part of our brain is activated, which tells our reacting brain to calm down. This is because gratitude decreases the level of the stress hormone cortisol, which we first mentioned in chapter 1 (Dunn 2015; Scott 2018a).

A teen once shared a great quote with me, which I happily pass on to you: "It is not happy people who are thankful; it is thankful people who are happy." People who often feel grateful and appreciative are happier, less stressed, and less depressed (Dunn 2015; Scott 2018a). The more you bask in what you have (versus what you think you *should* have), the happier you'll feel. That counterproductive "should" think-ing is a robber of gratitude! Evaluating and challenging those "shoulds" with healthier thoughts, such as ones that start with "I will try" or "I will work toward," as discussed in chapter 3, can really stimulate you to appreciate everything you already possess.

Once you start to take note of things you're thankful for, the more they'll stream into your awareness—just like a rushing waterfall, a cleansing rain, or a refreshing shower to wash away stress.

Try This! Taking a Gratitude Shower

You can help send your stress down the drain by stepping into an imaginary shower. Here's what to do: Simply close your eyes and picture the "good stuff" in your life raining down on you. Start with whatever comes to mind first. Perhaps you're grateful for your family or your friends. Think of everything you do together and all the experiences you've shared. Remind yourself of each person's good qualities, what you love about them, or why it means so much to you to have them in your life. Perhaps you're grateful that you get to take part in fun activities or pursue cool interests. What are they? Think about the enjoyment they bring you and how much they have to offer. What opportunities for learning, discovery, socialization, or personal improvement do they represent for you?

You don't need to limit yourself to the things you think you *should* be grateful for or what other people would say are the best things in life. Perhaps you're grateful for your brand-new record player, even though your friends are all about their iPhones. Or maybe you really love your iPhone. Perhaps you're grateful for those worn old books you read again and again, or you love reading them on your electronic device instead. Try to break down what you're grateful for into parts in some way. For example, you can be thankful for your favorite band and then be thankful for each band member, the various instruments that create the music, and the fact that you have eyes to see and ears to listen. You can be thankful for your team or your club and for each one of your teammates or friends. You can be thankful for your car, your car's cool stereo, and even its boring old engine, because without an engine it wouldn't be much use to you. You can also be thankful for that navigation app on your phone so you don't get lost, or being able to use your parents' phone to keep them from getting lost as well!

Stay in this shower as long as you want. I promise your parents or siblings won't yell at you to get out!

Afterward, reflect on the following questions:

How satisfying did it feel to notice the things in your life that you're grateful for?

Did being grateful leave you feeling emotionally fulfilled?

Did the initial images of the things you appreciate lead you to notice more things you appreciate?

Whether you're stressed out about school challenges, friend drama, or family hassles, a little gratitude can quickly put you in a more positive frame of mind. Getting into gratitude is a quick and easy stress-squelcher. Here's one more gratitude-based activity that you may want to hold on to for use during times of stress.

Try This! Grasping on to Gratitude

Do the following to get in touch with gratitude (pun intended, as you'll soon see).

Put out your hand, with your palm facing you and your fingers sticking up. Now simply think of something you're grateful for. Once you've got it, put your pinky down. Think of a different thing you appreciate, and put your ring finger down. As you think of three more things, put down your middle finger, your index finger, and your thumb. Congratulations—you've just grabbed a handful of gratitude! If you happen to be on a gratitude roll, and need more fingers, then keep going and use your other hand as well. You can even take a walk or go for a run while doing this activity, to help you leave your stress behind.

Afterward, reflect on the following questions:

How did it feel to fill your hand with gratitude?

Did using your fingers (instead of just your mind) make the things you're grateful for seem more tangible or more real?

Might you be grateful in the future for doing this quick activity any time you need to lower your stress level?

Further ways to get gratitude in your life include simply keeping a journal. If you elect to keep a journal, you can do so by writing your gratitude-related thoughts in a notebook. To help yourself get started on a gratitude journal, check out the Gratitude Tracker at http://newharbinger.com/43911. You can use it as a template for your journal or simply print copies and fill them in directly. When it comes to taking the time to practice a little gratitude, the more often you do it, the better you'll feel. However, don't pressure yourself or feel bad if some days you forget to write in your journal. You can simply do it whenever stress leaves you emotionally empty and depleted, to give yourself a pleasant feeling of how full your life is.

You might like to have a gratitude app instead, which can give you a periodic reminder (such as a notification alert) to stop what you're doing and think of a few things you're grateful for. Or you can keep a pebble in your pocket and, any time you reach into your pocket and feel it there, remind yourself of three things you're happy to have in your life. Or use any object you like, placed wherever you like, to help you get in touch with gratitude once in a while. Put a mug (a nice reminder that gratitude fills us) with the word "gratitude" written down and taped on it, a simple piece of jewelry with special meaning or just a coin, or even this book on your desk, and every time you look at it, tell yourself something you're grateful for.

Check out the following tidbits from teens who discovered the stress-lowering benefits of gratitude:

In Their Own Words

"My friends surprised me with this group text on my birthday. I wrote this in my journal to help myself realize how lucky I was to have kids who really care about me."
Darryl, age 14

"One day, I was all upset about learning this new gymnastic routine, and I was taking it out on my mom. Then I stopped to appreciate her taking me to all those meets and preparing refreshments for our team. It calmed me down to focus on that." **Alyssa, age 14**

"In social studies, I learned that, in many developing countries, people don't have clean water or enough food. I was like, 'For real?' I realized I needed to appreciate all I have in my life. It really added meaning to my gratitude shower, too!" **Bailey, age 16**

These teens all were able to make the connection that the more they brought gratitude into their lives, the more they slowed down their roller coasters of stress.

If you make the choice to have an attitude of gratitude by doing the activities in this chapter (or ones you come up with on your own) on a regular basis, your gratitude will snowball. That is, you'll perceive more and more things to be grateful for. For example, you may step outside and notice how the sky is beautiful on a particular day. That may lead you to think, *Wow, I'm totally lucky to be alive and enjoy this day!* Or you'll see someone you like and think: *It really is great when we hang out together. I really like how her positive energy helps me feel good too.* All you need to do is get the (snow)ball rolling. Pretty cool, right?

Putting It All Together

In this chapter, we looked at the concepts of flow and gratitude. By intently focusing on something that you really like striving to do, or an activity you can really lose yourself in, you can enter a state of flow in which the stressors in your life will feel much less bothersome. Gratitude can help you keep sight of the "good stuff" in your life, to leave you feeling more fulfilled. Both of these tools from positive psychology—tools, by the way, that I've taught thousands of teens like you to use—are great for managing stress.

In the next chapter, we'll be going back to school, so to speak. So stay strapped in for more opportunities to practice using your CBT and positive psychology brakes on the big, bad roller coaster of school stress.

PART 4

Using Your Brakes on Three of the Most Challenging Rides

chapter 8

Surviving Schoolwork Stress

In this final part of the book, we'll be bringing together stress-reducing solutions from CBT and positive psychology. Each chapter provides specific examples of stressful situations that could be similar to those you'll face, followed by a list of strategies meant to help you calm your reacting brain, use positive coping behaviors, and take action to overcome your challenges. The strategies are numbered, indicating which one you might use first, second, and so on. Although following all the steps would probably give you the greatest benefit, you don't have to use every single one that applies. It's unlikely that your problems will be exactly the same as these examples anyway. That's okay, because these stress-lowering strategies are highly applicable, even if your circumstances don't totally match the situations provided. With a little imagination, you can make them work for you. And remember, you don't always have to use your CBT skills and positive psychology at the same time. Use one or the other if that helps.

Feel free to make a mental note of the steps in the sections "Slowing down the roller coaster" that seem most appealing or that you'd be most comfortable with. The best strategies are the ones you're most likely to use! Other coping tools you see here, however, may later pop up in your mind when facing future challenges that come your way.

The point of these next three chapters is to help you generate ideas and to try to draw on a variety of skills that you've learned up to this point to help you handle all sorts of situations in three major areas of your life. In this chapter, we'll apply examples of using CBT and positive psychology skills for common sources of stress you might find at school. We're going to keep our focus here on managing stress that stems from academic demands. In chapter 9, which addresses stress related to social situations, we'll briefly "revisit school," touching on a few examples of peer-related social pressures that can pop up there as well. Chapter 10 will address stress related to family issues. Along the way, you'll also see those familiar Try This! activities to help you further reflect on managing stress.

Don't Let Stress Slip You Up

It's important to do your best in school. After all, a good education opens doors to opportunities for the rest of your life. My guess is you've heard that many times—maybe too many!

Do fears of not doing well in your classes weigh you down? Or do self-imposed, perpetual perfectionistic pressures make your head spin? Pressure to succeed in school, at times, can really feel demanding and overwhelming. Those crushing schoolwork demands just don't seem to stop. Just when you lunge though one big test or assignment on your roller coaster of stress, other challenges keep coming your way. The pressures that come from classwork, homework, tests, and presentations can rattle you big-time.

If you remember from chapter 1, a survey by the American Psychological Association found that teens report higher stress levels than adults during the school year (Bethune 2014). So if school stress is knocking you for a loop, just know that you're not alone! While some students are good at not showing it, most of your peers likely get stressed out over academic demands. Academic stress may manifest as worry, sadness, or anger. After a super-hard exam, have you ever heard mutterings like these? "That test sucked! It was sooo ridiculously hard!" "Man, I studied my butt off and it didn't even make a difference. I'll never pass this class!"

One teen told me his desired solution for school stress: make attendance totally optional, get rid of homework, be allowed to hang out all day with friends, and have the smartest kids do the classwork for everyone else. How does that sound to you? It would certainly lighten up your academic load, wouldn't it?

I'm sorry, but that is totally not happening. So put those daydreams aside and learn how you really *can* manage your school stress.

You Don't Have to Stress to Impress

Why is keeping the stress of your various school demands under control so important? High achievers have to push themselves to the breaking point, right?

No, not necessarily. You can do well in school *and* lead a less stressful life. Take a minute to compare the negative outcomes of unmanaged academic stress with the more beneficial outcomes of stress that's properly managed.

Unmanaged Academic Stress	Managed Academic Stress
Fuels negative thoughts about schoolwork, homework, and relationships with teachers	Creates more positive and helpful thoughts toward school-related situations
Increases feelings of anxiety, frustration, and sadness along with resistance/avoidance of schoolwork	Creates calm feelings and promotes a "can do" attitude toward school responsibilities

Unmanaged Academic Stress	Managed Academic Stress
Leads to frenzied cramming for quizzes, tests, and projects	Promotes proactively learning class material for solid quiz/test/ presentation preparation
Can result in physical symptoms including aches and pains, changes in eating habits, poor sleep, and even sleepless nights	Promotes better overall health and solid sleep
Can lead to emotionally shutting down or getting short-tempered with family and peers	Encourages emotional flexibility for managing school and non-school functioning

Can you see how your school-pressuring thoughts, feelings, and behaviors can be driven by stress? The good news is that learning how to manage these demands can help you not only in school, but also with your overall health and relationships with those around you.

I hope you'll maintain an open mind when learning to use your CBT and positive psychology brakes to keep you feeling in control with school stressors. All it takes is some willingness and practice using these skills, and school will be much less overwhelming. So when the bell rings for class to start, you'll be ready to roll! Let's start by looking at stress about your ability to succeed in the long term or in general.

Anxiety over School Performance

Stressful academic demands can look and feel different to various teens, depending on their previous experience, their goals, and their circumstances. Check out some examples:

* Greg, a high-school senior, had found his classes and homework to be super-challenging since way back in middle school. He was worried about getting enough credits to graduate.

* Noreen, another senior, desperately wanted to maintain her 4.4 grade point average (including weighted credits for her Advanced Placement classes) in hopes of getting into an Ivy League school.

* Lydia, a sophomore, felt super-stressed and wondered whether she had overloaded herself because she was taking advanced classes in geometry and biology at the same time.

* George, a freshman with a learning disability and attention issues, was about to start going to a public high school after years of being in private school. He was worried that the work would be harder in his new school, even though he was supposed to get academic supports there.

* Michelle, age thirteen, wanted to do really well in middle school to be eligible for advanced classes in high school, in order to improve her chances of getting into the US Naval Academy.

Your thoughts about demanding academic situations like these can make or break how you feel about them and determine what you do to cope. Check out what some teens have said about their academic demands and the counterproductive thoughts they struggle with related to school grades.

In Their Own Words

"Ugh, I'm so mad right now! I just got back my AP history test and I got an A minus. I know people say that's still good, but no one understands that it's not good enough for *me*."
Colleen, age 17

"I had a huge test coming up in my biology class. I thought I was all set, but then I heard some of the super-smart kids freaking out about it in the cafeteria. Then I started really worrying, and I was like, *Do I really even know this stuff?*"
Scott, age 16

"My parents constantly ask me how I'm doing in school! I'm sorry, but I just totally give them attitude. They think that asking me about my classes helps me or something, but all it does is stress me out even more!" **Hannah, age 14**

As you may recall, the chapter 3 activity Exploring Your Unhelpful Thoughts featured some examples of how to challenge negative, counterproductive thoughts about school performance. You may further remember that in chapter 4 we touched on situations that trigger academic worries. One example of those triggers is reflected above in Scott's quote about the comments he heard his peers make.

Check out a few brief examples of how to use CBT, along with positive psychology, for stress about your performance in school.

Situation: You're trying to study, but you just can't absorb the material.

Unhelpful thought: *Nothing I do helps. I'm always going to be lost.*

Slowing down the roller coaster:

1. Challenge your distorted negative thought (CBT skills, chapter 4). Tell yourself, *This is hard to understand, but I can keep trying.*

2. See if you can get into flow by stretching yourself to learn this new material and focusing on the aspects of it that you like or that you grasp most easily (positive psychology skills, chapter 7).

Situation: You're not sure how to do a particular assignment.

Unhelpful thought: *I'm so stupid! I can't understand this assignment.*

Slowing down the roller coaster:

1. Challenge your distorted negative thought (CBT skills, chapter 4). Tell yourself, *Not knowing how to do this does not mean I'm stupid.*

2. Recall other difficult assignments that you've figured out, feel gratitude for these past successes, and determine which of your strengths can help you (positive psychology, chapters 6 and 7).

Situation: Your paper for English class is overdue, and you haven't started it yet.

Unhelpful thought: *I keep trying to start this paper but just can't do it. I'm doomed.*

Slowing down the roller coaster:

1. Break a big task into manageable tasks (CBT skills, chapter 5): write your ideas on index cards, figure out how to link them together, and then write your first paragraph.

2. Optimistically see the missed deadline as a setback and not a failure. See this experience as a chance to build grit by pushing

through with determination to achieve a difficult goal (positive psychology, chapter 6).

Situation: You are fearful of seeking help from your teacher for developing an idea and getting her opinion on your possible sources for your research paper.

Unhelpful thought: *If I ask for help, my teacher will give me flak.*

Slowing down the roller coaster:

1. Reframe help-seeking as self-improvement versus self-shame (CBT skills, chapter 4).

2. See struggles and working on them as signs of strength and grit (positive psychology, chapter 6).

Can you see how using your CBT skills and positive psychology can help you calm down and manage school demands? Let's now look at some common situations of academic stress and ways of coping with them.

Keeping Up in Class

Have you found yourself not understanding what your teacher is talking about in class? Does it really stress you out?

When you can't keep up in class, you may wonder whether you'll ever understand the material. You may feel like everyone else is doing just fine, so what's *your* problem? Perhaps you begin to dread the inevitable test on this confusing stuff.

Situation: You're taking notes and can't follow what the teacher is presenting in her lecture because she's going too fast.

Slowing down the roller coaster:

1. Take a calming breath or two and challenge your "should" thinking (e.g., *I should be able to keep up*) with a "will try" attitude. You could think, *Even though this is tough, I'll more likely catch on if I keep trying to follow this lecture.* Can you see how this thought also promotes grit? For the negative comparison *Everyone else seems to be following this but me,* you could rethink it as, *Comparing myself to everyone else is a waste of energy that I can instead use for focusing on what the teacher is saying.*

2. Adjust your note-taking with a "less is more" mind-set by focusing on writing fewer hard-to-understand details and sticking mostly to the general ideas.

3. Empower yourself by giving yourself credit (a strength) to learn the material and realize that the teacher may not be aware of how fast she's going.

4. Consider speaking up and politely but assertively letting the teacher know she's going too fast for you. Or see her after class and express your concern. Ask her for help at this time if you might need it.

5. Use a mantra to inspire yourself, such as "Stick with it."

Homework and Studying Demands

Do you get overwhelmed by too much homework? Have you ever felt like you understood what was said in class during the day, yet once you started the homework you felt lost? Here are some ways to put the brakes on the stress that comes from homework demands.

Situation: Your teacher gives you a difficult homework assignment. At first, you think you can get it done without much problem, but once you dive into it, you realize it's going to be very time-consuming. Your mind races to all the other homework you still have to do, and you start to panic.

Slowing down the roller coaster:

1. Take a few deep breaths and count to ten.

2. Start "doing instead of stewing" by cleaning off your desk or making your bed (even if you're thinking *I'm just going to mess it up later, though!*).

3. Think optimistically about putting in the work, getting the assignment done, and earning a good grade on it.

4. Review the subject matter that the homework is based on.

5. Once you have a better grasp of the material (if you still don't, then reach out to a peer for help), set a timer for fifteen minutes to get yourself going on the assignment.

6. If you start to get unhelpful thoughts like *I'll never get this done* or *This assignment is totally ridiculous*, then tell yourself *I'll do it anyway*.

7. Tell yourself, *Yeah, I'm frustrated by all this work, but focusing on breaking it down and getting it done keeps me feeling in flow, which helps keep me calm.*

8. Know that you don't have to spend all night on one assignment, especially if you're getting stressed about other things you have to do. Less time (within reason!) may count for more.

Test Anxiety

Do you ever worry about taking quizzes, tests, or major exams? If you're like most teens, your roller coaster probably feels like it's spinning out of control for some of those tests. If you find yourself worried while cramming for a test, you may think, *I don't have time for stress management*. Trust me, though, that *really is* the time to manage your stressed-out feelings!

Situation: You have a math test tomorrow. You're doing some last-minute studying when you notice that you feel panicked.

Slowing down the roller coaster:

1. Take a centering, mindful breath. Then remind yourself of all the class material that you do know.

2. Reflect on past tests that you did better on than expected. This can give you a shot of renewed confidence.

3. Reflect on a sense of purpose to "own" the test (seeing the subject matter as cool or as helping you on the path to getting into a desired college). Embrace this sense of purpose to get into flow as you study.

4. Ask yourself what's the worst that can happen if you fail. Will you be sent to sit on top of the school roof in the rain while wearing a dunce cap? Probably not!

5. If you continue to doubt yourself, remind yourself that if you don't do well, you can do better next time.

6. Don't overstudy (less may be more), especially if it interferes with sleep. The more sleep you get, the better your thinking brain will be able to recall the information you'll need for the test.

Anxiety About Presentations

Knowing that you have to do a presentation can be very stress-inducing. How about actually standing in front of your class on presentation day? Public speaking alone is enough to make some teens and even adults nauseated. For days, your mind may be flooded with worries: *What if my mind goes blank and I don't know what to say? What if I make a fool of myself? What if my acne doesn't clear up in time and it makes me even more self-conscious?* The presentation-related roller coaster really can make anyone feel dizzy!

Situation: You've prepared a presentation, and you've gone through it a few times in the mirror, but now you're feeling overwhelmed the night before. You're worried you'll have a panic attack in front of your class.

Slowing down the roller coaster:

1. Practice in front of an audience (such as your siblings or parents). Notice how the passage of time starts to fade away and you feel a sense of flow by immersing yourself in what you have to say.

2. Hold a confident posture and optimistically visualize where you'll be giving your talk and how it'll go well. Feel strength from valuing *your* creative or particular way of sharing this information.

3. Reflect on your grit for pushing yourself to learn the subject matter amid all the other school demands you're facing.

4. Consider a mantra to reassure yourself, such as "I'm making this happen!"

5. Ask yourself, *What's the worst that can happen?* Even if you were to throw up all over the place (which is very likely *not* going to happen), wouldn't you still be able to have a good life?

6. As you practice your presentation, try to feel more optimistic and gain an increasing sense of flow—being in the groove—as you realize that each run-through makes you more prepared and will help you seem knowledgeable to your audience.

7. Remind yourself to smile at some peers you feel comfortable with on presentation day to help lower your anxiety.

8. Even though your peers will probably have no choice but to listen to you, try to have gratitude for their attention tomorrow. Plan to thank them for it. This can help you feel more confident.

Let's take a look now at Sharon, who used some of the above suggestions to get through a challenging presentation and even some disappointment about her grade on it.

Sharon's Story

Sharon had been worried for weeks about a slideshow presentation for her history class. The night before she was scheduled to do it, she didn't sleep well. While initially worried upon waking, she reminded herself how hard she had prepared for this day. She identified her counterproductive thought Mine will be the worst presentation of the class *and challenged this negative comparison/premature conclusion with the thought* It feels better reminding myself that my hard work got me here instead of obsessing about whether people will like my presentation. Even if some people don't like what I have to say, chances are that others will find it interesting. *She reminded herself of her strengths (self-discipline, good communicator). This helped her calm down. She further shifted from thinking it had to be perfect to becoming excited to do the presentation.*

The next day, when she gave her talk, she surprisingly felt a sense of flow, being astonished at how quickly the time went and how in the zone she felt.

Her teacher gave her an A minus on the presentation, commenting that she could've used fewer slides. When Sharon noticed the automatic negative thought: Ugh, he didn't like it after all. I'm so disappointed, *she challenged this negative filtering by reminding herself that her presentation didn't have to be perfect.*

Now let's turn to a stressful topic in the next section that I will no longer delay mentioning—procrastination!

Procrastination

Do you put off studying, homework assignments, long-term projects, and, if you're a high-school senior, college applications? Has putting off your schoolwork (perhaps in favor of going on social media, messaging your friends, or playing video games) ever led you to a lot of worries, aggravation, and even all-nighters? Have you maybe even taken out your procrastination-related stress and angst on your siblings or parents? If so, you're a card-carrying member of Club Procrastination. This is one roller-coaster ride that's worth skipping!

If you procrastinate, perhaps it's out of fear of not doing your schoolwork perfectly. Maybe you feel overwhelmed and stressed out from too many demands, so you rationalize that you "deserve" time to relax. Maybe you've counterproductively told yourself that you hate school or that you "just lack motivation." Or, you vaguely believe you'll "do it later," when you feel more up to it—but that time never comes.

Betsy's Story

Betsy had struggled with attention problems and worries about school for several years. When discussing an overdue school project she was anxious about, she expressed having the best intentions to catch up in school but said, "When it comes down to it, I just distract myself with all the ways I can to avoid getting my work done." Fortunately, Betsy learned some CBT strategies and was able to notice and dispute the counterproductive, self-defeating thought I'm just lazy and can't get anything done. *This enabled her to put forth effort instead of continuing to put things off.*

Let's now look at a procrastination situation and how to slow down this distressing roller coaster.

Situation: You've been avoiding writing a paper for English class for quite some time, and now it's overdue. You just saw your English teacher in the hallway, which made your stomach start doing flips. On the bus ride home, you feel hopeless about ever getting the paper done.

Slowing down the roller coaster:

1. Clean out your backpack or do some rote task to get into "doing" mode.

2. Tell yourself that motivation for the paper will come once you begin to work on it.

3. Reduce potential distractions: put your cell phone out of sight in case it buzzes or lights up with a message.

4. Develop a doable plan including selecting a topic, gathering sources, writing an outline, and committing to get these things done by a certain time.

5. Give yourself credit for showing some grit to work through your discomfort about this assignment.

6. Begin a short initial work session to make starting the paper less anxiety-provoking, and feel how your resistance is broken.

7. Reconnect with your intention and feel yourself being "all in" with a sense of purpose for doing the paper (e.g., to train and prepare yourself to write essays for college-level classes).

8. Feel positive about the benefits of completing the task to feel motivated. As you generate optimistic feelings, you'll feel less stressed, and this is a gift that keeps on giving. Notice how it feels good to appreciate your grit, which gets you to the other side—success!

Let's end this chapter with an exercise in optimism to help you become less stressed and more successful in school.

Try This! Visualizing Your Best School Performance

Imagine how letting go of catastrophic thoughts about schoolwork can leave you feeling better. Now picture being successful in school while becoming less stressed about it, and reflect on the following questions.

What have you done, and what are you doing, that can help you think more positively about your schoolwork?

How does focusing on your past successes in school improve your mood in the present?

Can you see how focusing on past successes and future positive outcomes inspires you to take action?

How does focusing on getting good grades in the future help you feel less stressed about your grades right now?

Putting It All Together

In this chapter, we discussed how school can really get you going on the roller coaster of stress. We then explored how you might practice your CBT and positive psychology skills to calm yourself and feel better about your academic struggles.

Now let's move on to those challenging social demands, where stress often rears its head as well.

chapter 9

Riding Out Friendship Frustrations and Dating Drama

Since you became a teen, your social relationships have become more complex. Have you noticed? It's because your maturing brain plays a role in making your friendships more involved. It processes and interprets all those experiences and thoughts about past social involvements, which drive your preferences for whom you can best relate to and connect with.

Hanging out with friends is usually pretty awesome. But when there are social disconnects, misunderstandings, or situations of drifting apart, friendships can feel quite stressful. You may find yourself wondering—even stressing—about what friends, acquaintances, and even virtual strangers really think about you.

And then there are intimate connections and relationships. Being in a relationship that feels good is wonderful. Having your relationship go through ups and downs, however, is a really rough roller coaster to be on. Then, when others are all up in your business about your boyfriend or girlfriend or your crush, that just adds stress. Breakups, when they occur, can be not only painful, but also super-stressful.

Learning how to deal with various types of social stress will help you feel calmer and happier. The focus of this chapter is on managing the ups and downs related to your friendships and other important social connections. The more you can keep your reacting brain under control by using your thinking brain with CBT skills and positive psychology, the less socially stressed you'll feel.

Check out the following exercise to get a sense of which, and how much, social stressors impact you.

Try This! Slicing Up Your Social Stress Pizza

If you're hungry to identify the social situations that create the most stress in your life, then let's turn to a great comfort food: pizza! But hold on. This exercise is not about eating pizza.

Get a sheet of paper and draw a big circle. Now draw a line across the center and another line cutting it right down the middle. Next draw two diagonal lines through the circle, like an X. You guessed it—you now have what looks like a pizza with eight slices.

Now check out this list of social stressors that all teens struggle with to some degree:

- Self-doubt

- Feeling left out or lonely in everyday life

- Not being in the popular group

- Jokes taken too far/being teased and bullied

- Gossip (that may or may not be true)

- Drama or pressure from a dating relationship

- Misunderstandings and conflicts with friends

- Feeling like an outsider or unwelcome on social media

Now fill in the slices of your social stress pizza by writing any combination of these eight concerns in the circle, to indicate how much of your time or how much of your mind each one tends to occupy. Maybe self-doubt creates eight slices' worth of stress for you. Or maybe gossip feels like a good half of your social stress, while your concerns about your dating relationship are a quarter, and a friendship that may be in jeopardy is another quarter. Perhaps all eight stressors seem about equal in your life, so each one makes up a single slice.

How does it feel to see where your social stress comes from?

What social stressors, if any, take up the most space on your "pizza pie chart"?

Would how you filled in this chart have been different a few weeks, a few months, or a few years ago?

If at least one of the eight stressors is currently not part of your pizza, how grateful are you for that fact?

You may want to do this activity again in a week and see if your social stress pizza changes. It helps to stay mindful of how social stressors impact you and how they can change in importance over time. That way, you can respond to new challenges more effectively.

Acknowledging your social stressors is a huge step in managing them. By the way, if you think all your peers are "fine," and they're not chowing down on social stress pizza too, then you're in for a surprise.

Here's what some teens had to say about their own insecurities, embarrassments, and frustrations despite looking "fine" to the people around them.

In Their Own Words

"All the dudes I hang with just look cool, like it [their coolness] just easily comes through for them. But I don't feel cool and no one thinks I am, which sucks because I feel awkward all the time, like I never fit in. I definitely try to hide it, though." **Cody, age 14**

"The hallways at school are like runways, 'cause all the girls look pretty and happy. Hopefully, no one can tell, but I get really self-conscious. Sometimes I feel a little dizzy in the halls and get thoughts that I don't look pretty enough or, like, my hair is bad." **Linea, age 15**

"All this gossip is going around because I hooked up with a guy who wasn't my boyfriend. I'm just hoping [that soon] someone else becomes the center of the drama. I'm so done with trying to pretend this crap doesn't bother me. It never ends!" **Becky, age 15**

"[Most of the time], I kind of keep my head tilted down and make myself unapproachable. I feel like if I try to talk to someone, they'll just brush me off, especially if it's a girl." **Oliver, age 16**

"This guy, a friend of mine, at first totally did not have a clue who I am. Once he got to know me, he told me he had been thrown off by my 'resting bitch face.' People don't get that I'm really just always self-conscious." **Chelsea, age 17**

> "Some kids joked with me—right to my face—that I looked like a school shooter. It really bothered me, but I pretended it didn't." **Fred, age 18**

In the rest of this chapter, we're going to devour that social stress pizza. By that, I mean we'll discuss how to conquer the eight social stressors mentioned in the activity you just did. Let's take a big bite out of socially related self-doubt first.

Frequent Self-Doubt

As Linea said above, school hallways can be a breeding ground for insecurities. Sometimes it probably seems as though everyone's looking at you and judging you. If your acne is worse than usual, or your boyfriend just broke up with you, or last night you missed a shot and cost your team the game, you're worried what people may think when they see you, right?

Feeling bad about yourself really speeds up your roller coaster of stress! Check out how self-consciousness got the better of Bryce and how he survived it.

Bryce's Story

Bryce was president of the student council, played trumpet in the school marching band, and was on the soccer and track teams. People told him that he and his girlfriend, Tina, were the "perfect couple." Life was good until it suddenly wasn't, and his roller coaster nearly flew off the rails!

What happened was that Bryce got dumped by Tina—after, it turned out, she had started seeing another guy. Following that embarrassment, Bryce felt totally self-conscious. What made matters worse was his self-imposed pressure to cover up the way he was feeling in order to still be that happy-go-lucky guy who made people laugh.

Now, though, he was consumed with thinking he was a loser and feeling as though he could no longer live up to people's image of him. On top of that, he felt weird for having thoughts at times about the meaning of relationships and the meaning of life in general.

One day his favorite teacher, Mrs. Santiago, noticed that he had lost much of his spark. She pulled him aside to check in with him. Bryce told her what was going on, and she said she understood because she had felt the same way after a breakup during her younger years. She also revealed that she still struggled with feeling self-conscious at times. Bryce felt supported and relieved. Mrs. Santiago then suggested that Bryce focus on his self-value outside of whether he had a girlfriend, see his breakup as a grit-building experience, and optimistically reflect on how other girls might now see him as even more real and approachable. These suggestions helped him focus more positively on himself. He passed on this tip a week later to a female peer (whose boyfriend had broken up with her). She highly valued the advice as well.

Check out these situations and solutions to learn how to handle your self-doubt.

Situation: You've been sitting with a group of friends at lunch for the past few months, but they seem to be losing interest in you. You start shutting down and saying less whenever you're with them. Inwardly you want to talk but don't really know what to say.

Slowing down the roller coaster:

1. Identify your counterproductive thoughts, such as *They all look so confident and I'm a mess, I'll never fit in,* and *I should always know what to say.* Challenge them with healthier self-talk, such as *Just because they look confident doesn't mean I'm not, Part of fitting in anywhere is accepting I don't have to be perfect,* and *So what if I feel uncomfortable? I still have good things to offer.*

2. Inwardly reflect on your past positive social connections and times when you successfully led a conversation with your friends. You can even reinforce these confidence-building rec-ollections with a positive mantra, like "I know my value."

3. Plan to reconnect with your lunch crew and, if your anxious feelings give you some jitters, tell yourself *I'll do it anyway.*

4. Take a deep breath, reflect on being assertive, and engage the group in a "less is more" way, such as by sharing a smile, making a supportive comment, or laughing at a joke and fol-lowing that up with a relevant comment or question.

5. Optimistically look for signs that your friends are glad you joined in again, realizing that they go through struggles with self-confidence like everyone else—even if they don't admit it. For all you know, they were wondering if you didn't like them anymore.

6. If you decide in the end to leave this friend group, look past that temporary setback in your quest to form lasting connec-tions. Imagine yourself making new friends with whom you can be even more true to who you really are!

Situation: You're supposed to go to a dance with your girlfriends. But the dress you wanted to wear no longer fits. Plus, you just discovered a huge pimple on your forehead. Now you feel disgusted. You want to blow off the dance and just message your girlfriends that you feel sick.

Slowing down the roller coaster:

1. Visualize a calming yet inspiring image—perhaps one from nature, such as a flower in a field—and take a few gentle breaths in and out.

2. Identify your counterproductive thoughts, such as *I'm totally ugly!* Challenge them with healthier self-talk, such as *This sure is not a great time for a breakout on my face, and yes my weight is up a bit, but I don't have to look perfect.*

3. Say an affirmation, such as "My true beauty comes just as much from within as from my appearance." In addition, encourage yourself to feel grateful to have friends who appreciate your inner beauty.

4. Remind yourself that you won't be the only one at the dance who has acne. Plus, concerns about appearance are a part of everyone's pizza. Maybe your girlfriends aren't happy with the way they look right now either, but they'll still be glad you're there, and you can support one another.

5. See this dance as a "grit opportunity" by making the decision to push through your self-doubts. Remind yourself of your purpose in wanting to go to the dance in the first place. Can you still have fun even if you don't look your best?

6. Dance to one of your favorite jams in your room. As you do so, strive for flow. Can the magic of the music lift your mood? Do you feel like you can have a good time at the dance?

7. Get into flow at the dance by deliberately connecting to the music and keeping cool conversations going with your date and/or your girlfriends.

Feeling Left Out or Lonely in Everyday Life

Many teens tend to be introverted and are comfortable spending long periods of time alone. Yet our brain is wired to generate good feelings when we experience a sense of connection with others. When we lose that sense, such as when we feel distant from people we care about, we can start to feel lonely or even abandoned.

Situation: You keep feeling you don't fit in with anyone at your school. Thinking that no one really knows you or even wants to get to know you, most days you feel kind of numb.

Slowing down the roller coaster:

1. Ask yourself if you're negatively comparing yourself with your peers. Challenge your negative comparisons by reminding yourself of your own appealing qualities and strengths.

2. Give yourself some credit for your willingness to explore these pages and open yourself up to ways of feeling less socially isolated. See this as a personal strength as well!

3. Make a list of family members, teachers, and peers you've had positive interactions with, and truly reflect on it. Realize this list counts!

4. Create new sparks of social connection. Go to a public place such as a store and make eye contact with and smile toward at least one person you don't know.

5. Look into a recreational or sports league, an art class, or a church group as a way to connect with people who share your interests and values.

6. Reflect on your interests/personal strengths and ask your school counselor if you can start a new club.

7. Work on your grit by connecting with a sense of purpose. If you value helping people, then volunteer to read to children, assist at a nursing home (you may like connecting with the younger staff there), or pitch in at your local library as a way to follow that purpose.

Not Being in the Popular Group

As discussed by psychologist Mitch Prinstein, popularity during elementary school years is based on likability. But in your teen years, popularity is based on status (Altschuler 2017). How much of your social stress pizza relates to how you "stack up" in terms of popularity?

A big part of managing social stress comes from feeling value within yourself versus from how popular you think you are. As you can see in the following situation, being hung up on your score on the popularity meter can make you feel empty inside.

Situation: One Saturday night you're talking to a peer, who mentions a cool party going on but says it's really just for a group of popular kids. You're shocked, because you thought you were one of the popular kids. And you're upset that you weren't informed about the party.

Slowing down the roller coaster:

1. Realize that keeping score of how popular you are may lead to negatively comparing yourself with others (as shown in Bryce's story).

2. Fill yourself with a sense of appreciation for the friends you already have. Hop in a quick gratitude shower.

3. Reflect on your personal strengths and value them. (You may want to revisit the activity in chapter 3.)

4. Think optimistically about the many opportunities you'll have to form social connections throughout your life.

5. Even if the winds of popularity are not blowing in your direction, think about the grit you gain by having your own sense of purpose as a unique individual, while having a strong posture, and holding your head high without needing the approval of the masses.

Jokes Taken Too Far/Being Teased or Bullied

Sometimes people make unpleasant remarks and try to disguise them as humor. Has someone ever said something that left you feeling really bad, even after they added "Just kidding"? Even if that person truly didn't intend to be hurtful, feeling put down can be very stressful. It can be upsetting to be on the receiving end of a not-so-funny joke.

Situation: You're sitting down for lunch with your friend in the cafeteria, and you pull out a card you wrote to someone you secretly like who's sitting a few tables over. You show it to your friend to ask his opinion of it. With a grin, he grabs the card and takes it over to your now not-so-secret crush. You start to feel panicky and begin to sweat.

Slowing down the roller coaster:

1. Take some gentle, mindful deep breaths, and count to ten to help you stay cool.

2. Dispute any distorted negative thoughts, such as *Everyone will think I'm pathetic!* using *I'm the one in charge of my pride, not them,* recognizing that you don't have to feel humiliated by your friend's behavior.

3. Assertively ask your friend what he expects to accomplish.

4. Empower yourself by thinking "less is more," and without overly justifying your request, ask your friend to go retrieve your card.

5. If your friend tells you that he was "just joking around," then assertively let him know you appreciate his intention but remind him that no one likes to feel embarrassed.

6. If your friend refuses to get your card, then walk over to your crush, smile, and assert with some humor, "My friend back there clearly needs to work on his impulse control and twisted enthusiasm for promoting me."

Gossip That May or May Not Be True

Gossip, whether face to face or on social media, may seem like fun, but it can really do harm. The "news" of peer problems and conflicts can, for better or worse, spread like wildfire and be very hurtful. Misunderstandings that get whispered down the lane can result in teens suddenly feeling betrayed or even abandoned by their friends.

Situation: You and the guy you like were seen leaning in closely and talking at a party. He'd told you he had just broken up with his girlfriend, but the next day you learned they were still together. Later you hear a nasty, ungrounded rumor that you had sex with him after the party. Now you're being blamed for his subsequent breakup with his girlfriend. Someone at school has even called you a nasty name.

Slowing down the roller coaster:

1. Breathe calmly, and visualize yourself as a tree being blown in the wind that bends but will not break.

2. Resist the temptation to beat yourself up with thoughts like *I shouldn't have been so gullible!* Challenge them with *Anyone can be deceived at times, but I'll work toward being less likely to fall victim to it in the future.*

3. Hold your head up, maintain good posture, and let others marvel at your self-pride.

4. Embrace knowing your value (as we discussed in chapter 4). This well help you avoid negatively comparing yourself with others at this time when you're feeling vulnerable.

5. See this as a growth experience to learn from as you witness the damage that gossip can cause.

6. Let those who stick by you and defend you know that you appreciate their loyalty and their resistance to believing gossip.

Drama or Pressure from a Dating Relationship

An intimate relationship is wonderful but also can take your roller coaster on ups and downs like never before. You may often have a fear of being hurt. Other stresses include trying to balance time with your partner with time for friends, family, and schoolwork. And let's not overlook dealing with insecure and jealous feelings.

Situation: Your boyfriend isn't responding to your most recent text message and doesn't answer when you call.

Slowing down the roller coaster:

1. If you're feeling vulnerable with feelings of self-doubt, reassure yourself that in ambiguous situations like these, anyone can struggle with not knowing what's going on. See acknowledging these vulnerable feelings as a strength, and let them guide you to reach out in an honest way to find out why there was no response. At the same time, keep in mind that "less is more" if you have truly come off as too dependent or have come on too strong.

2. When you do make contact, ask your boyfriend if anything has occurred. Be open to hearing if there was a legitimate reason

for his delayed response (e.g., a family emergency or him not being allowed to communicate for some reason).

3. Be willing to grow from misunderstandings. See them as setbacks rather than failures.

4. Realize that accepting challenges never means embracing being mistreated, such as being deliberately ignored. If this is what's going on, reflect on knowing your value.

5. If your boyfriend doesn't want to do his part to stay connected, then it may be best for you to assertively and healthily disconnect from the relationship. After breaking up, you may understandably feel sad or empty. But realize you can take a more optimistic view by learning from this experience and having more chances to reconnect with friends.

Here's one further exercise to help you practice managing upsetting thoughts and feelings that can occur in a relationship.

Try This! Managing Stress in Your Relationship

Take a few calming breaths. Picture yourself in a heated argument with your boyfriend or girlfriend. Reflect on how you feel hurt and/or angry. Maybe your girlfriend or boyfriend behaved less than trustworthily—and you reacted less than respectfully. Or vice versa: maybe it's you who's being mistrusted by your partner, and your partner reacted too harshly.

Identify what your thoughts and feelings are.

Which of your thoughts and feelings seem reasonable?

Which ones seem distorted, exaggerated, or counterproductive? You can refer to chapter 4 or the Distorted Negative Thoughts Summary Sheet at http://newharbinger.com/43911.

Come up with new thoughts that are more reasonable and positive and that emphasize your strengths, as well as the idea that you can work things out.

Can you see how slowing down and evaluating your thoughts can lead to healthier behaviors and better decisions within your relationship?

Let's move now to what you can do if you find yourself stressed out from misunderstandings and conflicts with peers.

Misunderstandings and Conflicts with Friends

Most teens don't like conflict. Unfortunately, conflicts, whether spoken or unspoken, will arise. Managing them by calming down and using effective coping behaviors will help you deal with them.

Situation: You mistakenly sent a group message about a gathering at your house, but you inadvertently included an acquaintance you didn't mean to invite. This person replied that she wants to come to the party. Ack! You want to be nice and just allow her to attend, but some of your friends are direct-messaging you that they really don't want her present, at least for this particular gathering.

Slowing down the roller coaster:

1. Center yourself with a few gentle breaths and count to ten.

2. Text back directly a sincere apology for your messaging error, and offer to discuss it on the phone or in person.

3. Identify what counterproductive thoughts you're having. Dispute any labeling (e.g., *I'm so stupid*), "should" thinking (e.g., *I shouldn't have been so careless*), or all-or-nothing thinking (e.g., *I always mess up*).

4. Remind yourself that this embarrassing mistake happens to many people at times.

5. Think like an optimist by attributing your mistake to being distracted by all the other stuff going on in your life, rather than to a personal shortcoming or incompetence.

6. Work on being more mindful by taking a pause before you respond to messages and to double-check the recipient(s) before you click Send.

Now let's discuss the stress of social media.

Feeling Like an Outsider or Unwelcome on Social Media

Social media can feel good as a means of connecting with friends and others. It's fun and exciting to "get liked" and to see what others are up to. But social media can also be a breeding ground for thoughts that you don't fit in, loneliness, and gossip, as well as the other social stressors we've discussed. Just keep your CBT and positive psychology skills handy when you're on social media.

Situation: You had a friend group you were chatting with for a few weeks each day after school. It was cool to see what everyone else was sharing, and you liked being part of this online experience. You then see on social media that there are pictures of a party with this group that you weren't invited to. Next, you realize you're no longer being included in the group chat.

Slowing down the roller coaster:

1. Remind yourself that social media can be a fertile ground for misunderstandings and disconnects. In other words, you may be jumping to conclusions that your friends intended to exclude you by not inviting you to the party.

2. Be assertive and reach out to the person in the group you feel the most connection with, in order to explore whether something you wrote was misinterpreted or misunderstood.

3. If you're calling yourself a "loser" or otherwise negatively labeling yourself, be kinder toward yourself.

4. Repeat this mantra: "Social media is just one part of my being a socially connected person. It does not define my value as a person."

5. Think of how you might feel toward a friend in this situation, and apply the same compassion to yourself. What words of encouragement would you give your friend? You may advise her, for example, to view this as a learning experience— an opportunity to practice handling disappointment—and encourage her to optimistically look for friendships that are closer and sturdier.

6. Realize that while social media can be fun, it can be a place that tempts people to be fake by making themselves look unrealistically happy and cool. Taking breaks from social media sites can feel freeing, because these sites tend to fuel a great deal of negative comparison that's based on appearances.

7. Consider hanging more in person with your friends versus hitting them up on texts or on social media chats. Seeing them in person can help you feel more connected to those special people who value you because they like you and not just because of the things you post.

Putting It All Together

Social stress can be found in many areas of teenage life. In this chapter, we talked about eight big ones, and you learned to use your CBT and positive psychology skills to manage them.

We're going to now turn to those stressful situations that can arise in families, so that you can better manage them as well.

chapter 10

Managing Family Ups and Downs

Your parents and your family are likely a strong source of support in your life. At the same time, family relationships can be stressful due to tensions and conflicts. You and your parents may have differences over who gets to call the shots when it comes to hanging out with your friends, taking care of your room, and handling your schoolwork and future plans. Adding to your lifelong trip on the family roller coaster, your siblings can be both entertaining and annoying. This makes for even more ups and downs.

This chapter is about using your brakes to slow down your reacting brain when you feel family stress coming at you. You'll gain some big-time patience and understanding for when you have those annoying power struggles with your parents and siblings. We'll briefly address common challenges of being an only child as well. We'll also take a look at stress and worries that come with parental separation or the loss of a loved one.

All families go through rough patches. But knowing how to manage those stressful family times will keep you less stressed out. Keep in mind that the better you can manage your emotions toward your family—the more reasonable and grown-up you seem—the more likely your parents will provide you increased freedoms and privileges.

Clashing with Parents for Independence

It can feel really stressful when you want more freedom from your parents than they seem willing to give you. As a teen, you probably want to make as many of your own choices as you can. And your parents probably want you to grow into a self-reliant, independent adult. Yet they worry about your welfare and safety. As a result of these struggles, your parents may do the following kinds of bothersome things:

* Be too much in your business by asking too many questions

* Jump to unfair conclusions

* Check your text messages or text you a lot

* Express concerns about your friendships or your intimate relationships

* Look waaay too often on the school website to check your grades

* Threaten to take things away

* Argue with each other

* Give you consequences that get in the way of you seeing your friends

* Subject you to a lecture when you just want to be left alone

Here's how some teens who felt "totally smothered" expressed their desire for space and freedom from their concerned parents.

In Their Own Words

"My mom tries to tell me it's not so much me she worries about but who I hang with. It sucks that she can't give me a break and trust that I have good judgment." **Walt, age 14**

"My parents freak out about stuff that's no big deal. They think that if I don't remember to take out the trash or turn off the light, then how will I be a responsible, safe driver when I'm sixteen? Seriously?" **Jerome, age 15**

"I totally can't wait to be independent and do what I want without my parents worrying and nagging me!"
Tatiana, age 16

"They act like I'm going to blow it and lose this scholarship I was promised by the college that accepted me. But I'm halfway through my senior year, and I want to have some fun." **Lamont, age 18**

Perhaps you can relate to the above quotes. It can be super-frustrating when you and your parents aren't on the same page, which may be more often than not! At the same time, it's a sure thing that the more you control your own reactivity when you're dealing with your parents, the calmer they'll feel and act toward you, which can go a long way to win you some compromises. Check out the following situation and suggested solutions for getting along better with your parents.

Situation: Your parents say you're being disrespectful when you speak to them. Yet giving them attitude seems to be the only way to get them to back off and give you space.

Slowing down the roller coaster:

1. Reflect on what you're saying to yourself about your parents. Are you being fair, or are you thinking in a counterproductive way?

2. Ask yourself whether the only way to get them to back off is really to be mean. Are you jumping to conclusions?

3. Remind yourself that anxiety likely lurks underneath the concerns your parents may strongly express. Realizing that your parents are human, just like you, can help you stay in touch with their value while also knowing your own. Is the ability to understand their concerns a strength that you can learn?

4. Ask yourself if there were times when your worries got the better of you and maybe you took it out on your parents. Just like you, their worries may come out in a way that feels intense, off-putting, or unreasonable, even though they mean well. If so, can you take some proactive steps to show them they don't need to worry about you so much?

5. Be optimistic that, once you and your parents can have calmer conversations, they'll feel more connected to you, which will help them be more comfortable relaxing their control over you. It may give you an extra dimension of compassion to see that, for a long time, you've been a child in their eyes (and wasn't that true?). In the same way that you've been struggling to let

go of unhelpful attitudes toward the things that stress you out, your parents may be struggling to let go of their old perceptions of you and to see you as more of a grown-up.

6. Odds are that your parents have your back in the end. Reflect on the short list of people who'll love you no matter what you do. Are your parents somewhere in that list?

When you're feeling upset about your parents' rules and restrictions, call on your CBT and positive psychology brakes to calm you.

Try This! Reducing Conflict with Your Parents

Imagine any situation in which you feel your parents are hindering you from doing something you want to do. What are your upsetting thoughts and feelings that come along with this situation? For example, *They just won't let me do anything!* Or *Mom always gets frustrated.* Or *This is why I don't want to be nice—because they're never nice to me.* Can you see the negative filtering and all-or-nothing thinking you may be doing?

What are some of the negative things you do (the sort of things your parents might label as "acting out") when your upsetting thoughts and feelings get the better of you? Do you slam doors? How about being sarcastic or giving your parents the silent treatment?

Can you see how being tuned in to your upsetting thoughts and challenging them will help you get along better with your parents?

If you can be flexible enough in your thinking to try to see things from your parents' perspective, is there a chance that they might make more of an effort to see things from yours?

What are some ways that slowing down your roller coaster might actually result in you getting more freedom? More time to hang with your friends? Increased trust of you to manage your schoolwork and grades? Being seen as ready to get your driver's permit when the time comes? Trusting you more to go to gatherings and parties and keep yourself safe? The more you keep your cool, the more your parents may support your independence.

Okay, now let's move on to your annoying (yet likely sometimes lovable) siblings.

Surviving Struggles with Siblings

For many siblings, teasing that starts as goofy and playful sometimes goes too far and leads to arguments and fights. Does this ever happen in your family? Another source of stress and frustration might be how much your younger sibling seems to get away with compared to you. On the other hand, if *you're* the younger sibling, a big source of stress can be the pressure of living up to your older sibling's accomplishments. You might also feel as though *you* have to suffer as a result of mistakes that *your sibling* has made. There are opportunities for unfairness on each loop of the sibling stress roller coaster.

Stress in sibling relationships can have many other triggers, too. Here are some irritating sibling behaviors that you may be able to relate to:

* Not respecting your privacy

* "Borrowing" your things without permission

* Bothersome bathroom habits and messiness

* Television and gaming-console time conflicts

* Hanging around too much when your friends visit, especially if you're the older sibling

---

In Their Own Words

"My older sister takes infinity showers—they last forever!" My parents say something, but then she just goes back to being a shower hog!" **Pauline, age 13**

"My older brother has some kind of drug problem, and my parents are all stressed out about him going to a rehab. I feel like I have to suffer [as a result of *his* issues] because everyone is freakin' stressed out!" **Denise, age 15**

"My parents keep babying my younger brother. Yeah, okay, he has anxiety issues, but it's ridiculous how they shelter him." **Mateo, age 16**

Wouldn't it be nice to not get sucked into powerful struggles with your siblings? Even if you can't keep them from saying or doing the things that drive you nuts, you can choose to respond differently by taking on an emotionally healthier perspective.

Situation: Your older sister has a whiny voice or is big on drama when she talks to family members (and you say to yourself: *She is ruining this family! I just can't take this!*). Or your older brother seems consumed with his girlfriend and is always checking himself out before she visits. Then they hog the couch for hours and it's awkward because they're all over each other (*This totally sucks! I can't even feel comfortable in my own house anymore because of him and his stupid girlfriend!*). Or your younger sister drives you up the wall in the midst of morning madness because she chews with her mouth open (*She's so disgusting! Ugh!*).

Slowing down the roller coaster:

1. Identify your upsetting thoughts and feelings about your sibling, and try to dispute them. Does she really *always* annoy you? Will he truly *ruin* your life? Can the patience you develop from this experience become a strength for you in the future?

2. To change up what you're focusing on with your annoying sib, offer to do something you can both enjoy, such as get mutually absorbed in a challenging board game or video game. Maybe you'll even feel a sense of flow as you play together.

3. Reflect on what you're grateful for with your sibling. Does he have some positive qualities that you benefit from (for instance, he helps with chores, helps you with schoolwork, and provides comic relief)? Is she teaching you great personal strengths, such as tolerance and acceptance? Can enduring and working through hassles to improve your relationship with your sib contribute to your grit-building skills as well?

4. Optimistically reflect on how your relationship will likely become closer in years to come. Lots of siblings become great friends in adulthood.

If you're an only child or want to understand some of the struggles of only children, check out the next section.

The Challenges of Being an Only Child

If you're an only child, you likely have a lot of conversations with your parents. They may always be there for you to lend a hand or listen when you want them to. They have high expectations of you and help you do your best. But, at the same time, you may find all that attention to be smothering. And there's no sibling around to take the pressure off you.

Your peers who come from large families may think you're lucky to not have siblings intruding on your personal space; yet being an only child might feel a bit lonely at times. Perhaps you're sick of being told by jealous friends how great it must be to have your parents' attention all to yourself, as though the time you spend with your parents is filled with nothing but happy moments.

Check out the following quotes from teens without siblings.

In Their Own Words

"I love my parents, but it's boring not having another kid to hang out with when we go on vacation, so I really like when my parents let me bring a friend." **Oscar, age 15**

"It's so weird that people think I'm spoiled because I'm an only child. I use my money from my job to buy things, and I know many kids with siblings who [unlike me] get everything handed to them." **Taylor, age 16**

"My parents constantly want me to be perfect at everything."
Andy, age 18

If you can relate to any of the challenges these teens describe, the following activity may help you begin to see things in a different way.

Try This! Thinking Positively About Being an Only Child

Reflect on your experiences being an only child, and consider the following questions.

What are your thoughts about being an only child that might be counterproductive?

What are some more helpful and healthy thoughts you can use to challenge your counterproductive thoughts?

What are some strengths you may possess as a result of being an only child?

Does having friends help make up, in one or more ways, for not having siblings?

What opportunities are you grateful for that you might not possess if you had to share your life and your family's resources with a brother or sister?

Dealing with Feelings Related to Divorce

If your parents are divorced or going through divorce, the sheer weight of all the uncertainties in your life may feel crushing and seem like it'll never go away. You may be concerned that any time your parents are around each other (such as at your birthday parties, school performances, other special events, or even pickups and drop-offs), there'll be unspoken tension or they'll end up arguing. You may worry about changes in the custody schedule that could impact your ability to see your friends. Your entire living situation may be up in the air. Maybe one of your parents is in a new relationship or you have a stepparent, and there's some strain between you and this person you've had to let into your life. You may have had to get used to older stepsiblings or younger half-sibs. On top of all that, perhaps you're feeling pressure to make one or both of your parents happy. Or you're holding a lot of anger or resentment toward them—perhaps for unloading their troubles onto you, putting you in the middle, or forcing you to pick a side.

There's no shortage of reasons to want to complain about divorce stress. Just listen to these teens:

In Their Own Words

"My stepsister is mean and ignores me. I wish things were back to normal, with just my mom and my little brother living with me." **Bruce, age 13**

"I'm sick of being in the middle. My parents act like they're in middle school by behaving the way they do." **Kelly, age 14**

"My mom trashes my dad all the time, [and] my dad says Mom takes all the money. It's ridiculously confusing and hard to listen to." **Brad, age 15**

"I guess it was probably best for them to get a divorce, but I'm the one suffering the most. Like, my mom is really preoccupied with dating, and my dad buries himself in work for his job." **Paulina, age 16**

> "My parents get along really well. It's crazy, because while I don't want to see them fighting, it's confusing because sometimes I wonder why they even got divorced."
> **Curtis, age 17**

Check out the following activity to start to slow down the roller coaster of thoughts and feelings related to your parents' separation or divorce.

Try This! Coping with Divorce Stress

Reflect on memories of your family prior to your parents' separation or divorce. Think of the times spent together, family traditions, and the ways you used to see and communicate with your parents. Now consider your thoughts and feelings about how your parents' divorce will impact you.

Which upsetting feelings seem to be fueled by counterproductive thoughts?

Can you see how these negative thinking patterns will likely make this time of uncertainty even more difficult for you than it has to be?

Are there any ways you can see your parents' divorce more optimistically? For example, perhaps you'll enjoy more time alone with each parent.

Could becoming aware of peers from divorced families who are coping okay help you feel more optimistic that you can handle it too? If so, you can bring up the topic to your school counselor, put out some feelers among your friends to see if anyone has been in your situation, or search online for local groups for children of divorce. You may consider online forums (with appropriate cautions), or outside individual counseling, if this option is available to you.

Can preparing yourself to focus on healthily supporting both of your parents and handling this new twist in your family life become an opportunity to gain grit?

Can you feel a sense of flow in creating new activities or traditions with each parent, such as going on hikes or walks, having stimulating conversations during morning rides to school, or enjoying Sunday-night chats over a board game?

Now that we've discussed managing stresses that come with divorce, here's some help for you to get through the difficulty of losing a parent or other loved one, should that ever happen.

Coping with Loss

Feelings about the death of a family member can vary, but the common theme is an overwhelming sense of loss. If you ever have to suffer the loss of a parent, a sibling, a grandparent, an aunt, an uncle, or even a friend, it's important to realize that feeling sad, scared, or lonely is a normal reaction.

Different people mourn in different ways. There's no "right" way of reacting for someone dealing with a loss. For example, although crying is a normal expression of the sadness of loss, not crying is okay too. If you don't cry, you may have other ways of showing your emotions, such as wanting to be alone, feeling irritable, or even feeling a sense of relief (such as if the deceased person had been suffering from a painful illness).

On the other hand, it may seem better to stuff down your feelings. Making your loss seem like less of a big deal than it really is, or denying it even bothers you, is certainly one way of getting through the hardest moments. Trying to ignore the pain of loss, however, won't make it go away. In fact, turning away from your feelings can make you feel worse in the long run. And, in the short term, it can lead people to think that you don't need or want support.

Just know that it's normal to grieve. Letting go of "having to be strong" can help you accept and explore your grief-related feelings. You can choose to grieve in whatever way feels natural or fitting to you. If you've lost a loved one, even if it happened a long time ago, check out the activity below to open yourself up to grieving.

Try This! Feeling Loss in a Healthy Way

Gently reflect on the person who is no longer with you. Think about what you valued about this person. Also realistically consider their shortcomings. Think of the sights, sounds, smells, and other things that remind you of this person. As you hold these memories in your mind, take a few gentle, mindful breaths. Then ask yourself:

- What thoughts and feelings can help you view this loss in a healthy way?

- What counterproductive thoughts and associated feelings, such as thinking self-critically or pessimistically, may pressure you and get in the way of grieving (e.g., *I should have done more. Or I'll never be able to move on*).

- What have you learned about yourself as you've been grieving this loss? For example, that your ability to handle loss is stronger than you anticipated. Or that life's many twists and turns can give you opportunities to reflect on what and who you value, including your own life.

195

- Are you allowing yourself to see the positive ways you may be managing your grief, such as by honoring the lost person's legacy (perhaps by writing a short story, journaling, or with a drawing), participating in a walk or a run for a relevant charity, or reaching out to others for support (and perhaps to support others as well)?

- Can focusing on what you learned from this special person, or the treasured memories of your time together, help you feel ongoing gratitude for her or him?

Reflect on what else you've learned about yourself in relation to this loss. Have you made peace with what happened, or is there still more to understand about how it impacted you? Realize that ongoing questions about why a loss occurred, or what it may mean to you as you go forward, are a normal part of the grieving process. Sometimes realizing you don't have to have all the answers is the best way of coping with things that take a long time to process and fully comprehend.

Putting It All Together

You now have used your CBT and positive psychology brakes to keep you in control when you find yourself on the roller coaster of family stress. Despite squabbles and tensions, your family is always there for you. Managing your stressful feelings will go a long way toward helping you value the good times with them going forward.

In the next and final chapter, we'll discuss ways to maximize success with using your new stress-management brakes for the rest of your life. Unlike other brakes that wear down and eventually need to be replaced, your CBT and positive psychology ones will continue to regenerate and even get stronger the more you use them.

Final Words

Stress Management for Life

I hope you feel good about making it to the end of this book. We've discussed what causes stress and how it can impact you. You've learned CBT and positive psychology strategies to help you manage stress at school, in social situations, and in your family life. This brief final chapter will offer some thoughts on dealing with stress in your life going forward.

To sum up, the three big ideas you should take away from this book are:

* The way you think about stress impacts how you experience and cope with it.

* You can change the way you think, feel, and behave in response to stress.

* The more you effectively cope with stress, the easier it'll be to control it.

Your CBT and positive psychology brakes will last you for a lifetime. All you need to do to keep them in working order is to keep pulling those levers. Just remember that it is not realistic to eliminate all of your stress. The key is to keep your stress at lower levels so you can stay aware of demands and challenges that you encounter and be able to tackle them.

When stressful situations come your way, remember that you do have a choice as to which path you can take for handling them. The familiar path for many people, unfortunately, is to let stress negatively influence them. They spin along on the roller coaster of ruminating, complaining, negatively acting out, or feeling helpless. Your new path, however, is to manage stress so that *it* doesn't manage *you*.

There's a recent concept in brain science called neuroplasticity. Neuroscientists, who study the brain, used to think that our neurological makeup was more or less established in childhood and, after that, we were stuck with particular ways of thinking, feeling, and acting. But now we know that these connections aren't set in stone. In the same way that plastic can be reformed, reshaped, or remolded, our brains can be rewired. By putting in effort to overcome our challenges and unhelpful habits, we can create new, more helpful neural connections and strengthen them through practice. Then our old ways of thinking, feeling, and behaving become weaker and less automatic. In the beginning, it's easy to fall back into our old ways, but as time goes on, our new ways can become second nature. This concept comes into play when you think of the path to controlling your stress.

Imagine that for years you've been walking through a grassy field in a consistent way, and your footsteps have worn a path—the feeling stressed-out path. Even though the terrain is difficult—you have to climb over rocks and sometimes risk twisting your ankle on the bumpy ground—it seemed to be the only way of making your way through. But now, having read this book and taken the concepts to heart, you've begun to walk through that field by a different route. You've created a new path of coping with stress. This road is much smoother, and the obstacles seem smaller and easier to handle.

It may not feel easy at times to stay on this new path. Maybe peers around you are walking around saying negative things or acting stressed out. You may feel pulled toward them and start to go back down that old, familiar path of counterproductive thoughts that leads you right back to feeling out of control on the roller coaster of stress.

Learning to keep your stress-management brake levers handy may feel challenging at first. After all, the old path of getting yourself stressed out is where your reacting brain tells you to go. But, with the guidance of your thinking brain, your reacting brain will influence you less and less. By consistently using CBT skills and positive psychology, you'll establish new neural pathways for helpful thoughts to challenge your counterproductive thoughts faster and more powerfully. As this happens, that well-worn path of overreactivity within your brain will start to become far less recognizable because of emerging, rich green growth covering it up. Sometimes you'll likely start to go down that old, familiar path once again, but this time you'll realize it's taking you in the wrong direction, and now you have the choice to change paths. How cool is it that *you're* the one who'll be creating and nourishing new healthy pathways of managing stress in your life and feeling calmer and happier! And who knows—the people around you might start to walk along with you on your new path after they see how much better it makes you feel.

Seeing Setbacks in a Healthy Way

One of the best ways to manage your stress is to manage your expectations. Yes, it would be great for all of us to stay on top of upsetting thoughts every single time. But our daily lives are filled with distractions and time pressures that make it easy to get swept onto that fast-moving roller coaster of irrational, upsetting thoughts.

So keep in mind that just because your roller coaster starts to spin out of control doesn't mean you can't still pump the brakes. Just as you now know that you don't have to be perfect, you also don't have to use your brakes perfectly all the time for them to be valuable.

If you ever start to think *I just can't handle stress! I tried CBT skills and positive psychology, but they don't work for me*, remember that learning to manage your thoughts and feelings takes practice. In the words of one self-help expert, "Thinking is a habit, and like any other habit, it can be changed; it just takes effort and repetition" (Eliot 2015, 17). The more you identify your counterproductive thoughts and replace them with more reasonable, helpful thoughts, the calmer and happier you'll feel. You'll also make wiser decisions, because you'll be using your thinking brain instead of your reacting brain.

Your roller coaster of stress will still take you on some twists and turns in life. But with your new CBT and positive psychology skills, you now have super-effective ways to cope with challenging times. So when you feel like the ride's getting too crazy, just remember—you're the one in control!

Acknowledgments

A special thanks to Elizabeth Hollis Hansen, my acquisitions editor, for believing in me for this project. The editorial staff at New Harbinger Publications, including Vicraj Gill, Clancy Drake, and Heather Garnos, are highly dedicated and great at what they do. I am grateful for their valuable, supportive input and guidance. Freelance editor Will DeRooy, of Intelligent Editing, did a stellar job of helping me refine the manuscript. I could never have found my voice without his expert, thoughtful, and diligent assistance. His suggestions were right on target in terms of content and style. Thanks as well to my wonderful loving partner, Marina, for being patient as I toiled away on this project. A shout-out of gratitude also goes to my daughter, Gabby, for reviewing my content on academic, social, and family stressors in teens and providing me valuable feedback.

In closing, thanks to everyone who helped me work through my own counterproductive, stressful thoughts and feel proud of this book!

Resources

New Harbinger Publications *Stress Survival Guide for Teens*
web page

http://www.newharbinger.com/43911

This web page provides the following downloadable supplements
and worksheets that can be used with certain activities in the book:

* *Personal Strengths Summary Sheet* (Seeing Your Strengths, chapter 3)

* *Bodily Symptoms Tracker* (chapter 2)

* *Common Stress Triggers Summary Sheet* (Identifying Your Stress Triggers, chapter 4)

* *Distorted Negative Thoughts Summary Sheet* (Noticing Your Negative Thoughts and Feelings, chapter 4; Evaluating Your Negative Thoughts, chapter 4; Managing Stress in Your Relationship, chapter 9)

* *Tracking Bodily Symptoms and Counterproductive Thoughts and Feelings* (Noticing Your Negative Thoughts and Feelings, chapter 4)

* *Challenging Your Distorted Thoughts* (Challenging Your Distorted Thoughts, chapter 4)

* *Gratitude Tracker* (Grasping on to Gratitude, chapter 7)

and the following audio recording:

* *The Body Scan* (Brief Body Scan, chapter 2)

My website

http://www.drjeffonline.com

Contains more helpful information for teens.

KidsHealth Teen Site

https://kidshealth.org/en/teens/stress.html

Provides helpful stress-management tips for teens and audio meditations including Smiling Breath, Finger Count Breathing, and Belly Breathing.

Lifespan Emotinal Behavioral Health

https://www.bradleyhospital.org/

managing-stress-teens-and-adolescents-guide-parents

Contains helpful stress-management information for teens and tips for parents to help teens manage stress.

Palo Alto Medical Foundation

http://www.pamf.org/teen/life/stress/7stresstips.html

Provides information on general health, drugs and alcohol, emotional health, and sexual health.

Further Reading

Mary Karapetian Alvord and Anne McGrath, *Conquer Negative Thinking for Teens: A Workbook to Break the Nine Thought Habits That Are Holding You Back* (Oakland, CA: New Harbinger Publications, 2017).

Jeffrey Bernstein, *Letting Go of Anger: 54 Cards to Help Teens Tame Frustration,* (Eau Claire, WI: PESI, 2017).

Jeffrey Bernstein, *Mindfulness for Teen Worry: Quick and Easy Strategies to Let Go of Anxiety, Worry, and Stress* (Oakland, CA: New Harbinger Publications, 2017).

Gina M. Biegel, *The Stress Reduction Workbook for Teens: Mindfulness Skills to Help You Deal with Stress,* 2nd ed. (Oakland, CA: New Harbinger Publications, 2017).

Richard P. Brown and Patricia L. Gerbarg, *The Healing Power of the Breath: Simple Techniques to Reduce Stress and Anxiety, Enhance Concentration, and Balance Your Emotions* (Boulder, CO: Shambhala, 2012).

Lisa M. Schab, *The Anxiety Workbook for Teens: Activities to Help You Deal with Anxiety and Worry* (Oakland, CA: New Harbinger Publications, 2008).

Jennifer Shannon and Doug Shannon, *The Anxiety Survival Guide for Teens: CBT Skills to Overcome Fear, Worry, and Panic* (Oakland, CA: New Harbinger Publications, 2015).

References

Altschuler, Glenn C. 2017, July 12. "The Perils of Popularity." *Psychology Today.* https://www.psychologytoday.com/us/blog/is-america/201707/the -perils-popularity

Beck, Judith. 2018. "Definition of CBT" (video). Psychwire. https://psychwire .com/beck/resources/definition-of-cbt

Bergeisen, Michael. 2010, September 22. "The Neuroscience of Happiness." *Greater Good Magazine.* https://greatergood.berkeley.edu/article/item /the_neuroscience_of_happiness

Bethune, Sophie. April 2014. "Teen Stress Rivals That of Adults." *Monitor on Psychology* 45 (4): 20. http://apa.org/monitor/2014/04/teen-stress.aspx

Dunn, Lauren. 2015, November 26. "Be Thankful: Science Says Gratitude Is Good for Your Health." Today. https://www.today.com/health/be -thankful-science-says-gratitude-good-your-health-t58256

Eliot, John. 2015. *Overachievement: The Science of Working Less to Accomplish More.* New York: Diversion Books.

Emmons, Robert. 2010, November 16. "Why Gratitude Is Good." *Greater Good Magazine.* https://greatergood.berkeley.edu/article/item/why_gratitude _is_good

Gladwell, Malcolm. 2008. *Outliers: The Story of Success.* New York: Little, Brown.

Grohol, John M. 2019, January 17. "15 Common Cognitive Distortions." Psych Central. https://psychcentral.com/lib/15-common-cognitive-distortions

Holland, Judy. 2015, March 9. "Grit: The Key Ingredient to Your Kids' Success." *On Parenting* (blog). *Washington Post.* https://www.washingtonpost.com/news /parenting/wp/2015/03/09/grit-the-key-ingredient-to-your-kids-success

Jacques, Renee. 2013, September 25. "16 Wildly Successful People Who Overcame Huge Obstacles to Get There." *Huffington Post*. https://www .huffpost.com/entry/successful-people-obstacles_n_3964459

Jordan, Michael. 1994. *I Can't Accept Not Trying: Michael Jordan on the Pursuit of Excellence*. San Francisco: Harper.

Mayo Clinic Staff. n.d. "Stress Relief from Laughter? It's No Joke." Mayo Clinic. https://www.mayoclinic.org/healthy-lifestyle/stress-management/in -depth/stress-relief/art-20044456

McRaven, William. 2017, August 17. "If You Want to Change the World, Start Off by Making Your Bed—William McRaven, US Navy Admiral" (video). Goalcast.com, https://www.youtube.com/watch?v=3sK3wJAxGfs #t=0m25s

Munchies. 2015, December 7. "Legendary Rock Climber Alex Honnold's Vegetarian Diet" (video). https://youtu.be/ncDFDz9k35o#t=5m25s

Scott, Elizabeth. 2018a, October 4. "The Benefits of Cultivating Gratitude for Stress Relief." Verywell Mind. https://www.verywellmind.com /the-benefits-of-gratitude-for-stress-relief-3144867

———. 2018b, November 5. "The Health Benefits of Laughter." Verywell Mind. https://www.verywellmind.com/the-stress-management-and-health -benefits-of-laughter-3145084

Jeffrey Bernstein, PhD, is a child, teen, and family psychologist with over thirty years' experience. He completed his postdoctoral internship at the University of Pennsylvania Counseling Center, and holds a PhD in counseling psychology from the University at Albany, State University of New York (SUNY). He has appeared on the *Today Show*, *Court TV*, and more. He is author of *Mindfulness for Teen Worry*, *10 Days to a Less Defiant Child*, *10 Days to Less Distracted Child*, *Liking the Child You Love*, and *Why Can't You Read My Mind?* He also published the *Letting Go of Anger Card Deck*. He lives in the Philadelphia, PA, area.

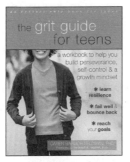

Register your **new harbinger** titles for additional benefits!

When you register your **new harbinger** title—purchased in any format, from any source—you get access to benefits like the following:

- Downloadable accessories like printable worksheets and extra content

- Instructional videos and audio files

- Information about updates, corrections, and new editions

Not every title has accessories, but we're adding new material all the time.

Access free accessories in 3 easy steps:

1. Sign in at NewHarbinger.com (or **register** to create an account).

2. Click on **register a book**. Search for your title and click the **register** button when it appears.

3. Click on the **book cover or title** to go to its details page. Click on **accessories** to view and access files.

That's all there is to it!

If you need help, visit:

NewHarbinger.com/accessories

new harbinger
CELEBRATING
40 YEARS